Amazing

BRAIDS &

BEADS

Pretty things
to make and do!

HH
HERMES
HOUSE

First published in 1999 by Hermes House

Hermes House books are available for bulk purchase for sales
promotion and for premium use. For details, write or call the sales
director, Hermes House, 27 West 20th Street, New York,
NY 10011; (800) 354-9657

Hermes House is an imprint of Anness Publishing Inc.

ISBN 1-84038-354-2

The activities and projects in this book were created by:
Petra Boase – *Friendship Bracelets, T-shirt Painting
and Modelling Fun*
Thomasina Smith – *Modelling Fun*
Jacki Wadeson – *Fabulous Hairstyles*

Publisher: Joanna Lorenz
Managing Editor, Children's Books:
Sue Grabham
Editors: Lyn Coutts, Louisa Somerville
Photography: John Freeman, Tim Ridley
Design: Axis Design
Additional design: Caroline Grimshaw

Previously published as part of a larger compendium, *The Really
Big Book of Amazing Things to Make and Do* and *The Outrageously
Big Activity, Play and Project Book.*

Printed in Hong Kong / China

10 9 8 7 6 5 4 3 2 1

Foreword

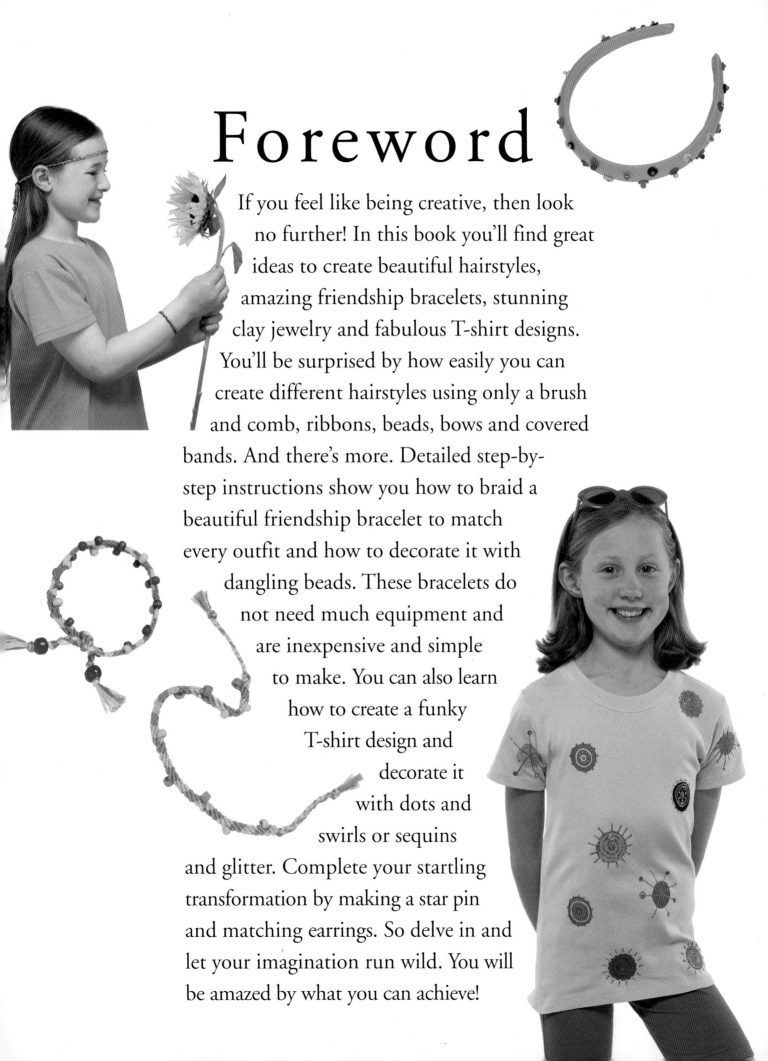

If you feel like being creative, then look no further! In this book you'll find great ideas to create beautiful hairstyles, amazing friendship bracelets, stunning clay jewelry and fabulous T-shirt designs. You'll be surprised by how easily you can create different hairstyles using only a brush and comb, ribbons, beads, bows and covered bands. And there's more. Detailed step-by-step instructions show you how to braid a beautiful friendship bracelet to match every outfit and how to decorate it with dangling beads. These bracelets do not need much equipment and are inexpensive and simple to make. You can also learn how to create a funky T-shirt design and decorate it with dots and swirls or sequins and glitter. Complete your startling transformation by making a star pin and matching earrings. So delve in and let your imagination run wild. You will be amazed by what you can achieve!

Contents

Friendship Bracelets

Petra Boase

Introduction

Friendship bracelets are a symbol of friendship, which is why they make such great presents for your friends and family. You could make matching friendship bracelets for you and your best pal, or weave a bracelet, anklet or necklace using the colors of your favorite sports team. But there is one more good thing about friendship bracelets—anyone can wear them—teenagers, young children and even adults!

Make them anywhere

Braiding and weaving friendship bracelets can be done anywhere—outside in the garden, on vacation, at the kitchen table or at friends' houses. You do not need to carry around big bags of equipment—all you need are threads, tape, scissors, beads and a smooth work surface. This means that friendship bracelets are also very inexpensive to make.

It is a good idea to store your braiding materials in a bag or small box. This will keep everything clean and ready for when you want to have some fun.

This Hippy Headband is made using the same braiding techniques that are used to make friendship bracelets.

Practice makes perfect

Some of the bracelet designs we show you are quite complicated. They may use many threads, and the knotting and braiding techniques may be a little tricky. But there are also many designs that even novice braiders will be able to perfect the first time around.

If you are having trouble making a particular bracelet, do not give up—try again after reading the instructions through and looking closely at the photographs. Your patience will be rewarded when you wear your own handmade bracelet and all your friends want to know where you bought it!

Experiment with colors

Once you have the knack of braiding and beading, let your imagination run wild and design your very own range of jewelry and accessories. You will soon be experimenting with your own combinations of colors and adding beads and decorations to your bracelets. You will also discover lots of new and exciting threads that will add unusual textures to your designs.

It is very easy to knot colorful beads into friendship bracelets and necklaces.

Materials

These are the materials and tools you will need to complete the following projects.

Barrette This hair accessory has a metal clip that grips the hair. The top of the barrette is made of plastic.

Beads These come in a wide variety of different sizes, colors, textures and patterns. Tiny or small beads usually have very small holes, so it is easier to thread them onto fine sewing thread, or to sew them onto items using a needle and thread. Medium- and large-size beads are perfect for using with thicker yarns. Metallic beads are shiny and add an extra sparkle to your handiwork.

Cotton knitting yarn This type of yarn is very chunky. Use cotton knitting yarn when you want to make a thick bracelet or anklet. It is available in many bright colors.

Electrical tape This is a strong tape. It is very good for fastening threads to a work surface. You can buy it at electrical and hardware stores.

Jewelry clamp A jewelry clamp can be fastened over the knot at each end of a friendship cord to finish it off. Jewelry fasteners can be attached to clamps.

Jewelry fastener This is a releasable metal clasp that can be used to secure a bracelet or necklace.

Metal rings These small metal loops are used to attach jewelry fasteners to jewelry clamps.

Pliers Use small jewelry pliers or needle-nosed pliers to open and close metal rings and to secure jewelry clamps. Many types of pliers have a cutting edge, so always ask for adult help when you use pliers.

Soft embroidery floss This is a thick thread that is ideal for friendship bracelets. It comes in many vibrant colors.

Stranded embroidery floss As its name suggests, this cotton thread is made up of many strands. It is very good for making patterned and knotted friendship bracelets.

Sunglasses attachments These rubber loops are used to attach sunglasses to a strap. Buy them at specialty bead shops.

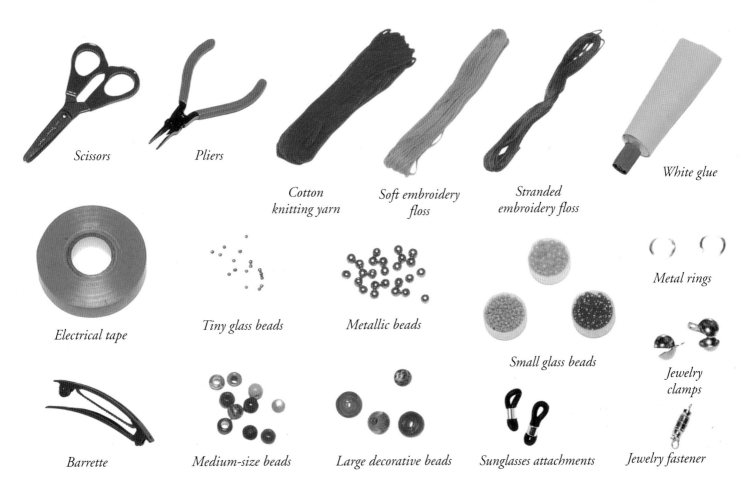

Scissors

Pliers

Cotton knitting yarn

Soft embroidery floss

Stranded embroidery floss

White glue

Electrical tape

Tiny glass beads

Metallic beads

Small glass beads

Metal rings

Jewelry clamps

Barrette

Medium-size beads

Large decorative beads

Sunglasses attachments

Jewelry fastener

Basic Techniques

Starting off

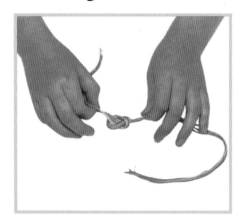

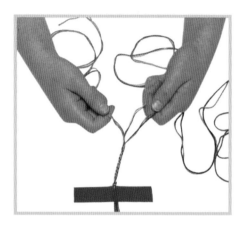

1 Cut the threads to the required length. Check that you are using the right type of thread and have the correct number of threads in each color. Gather the threads and line up the ends. Tie the threads together with a knot near one end. Each project will tell you exactly where to tie the knot.

2 Secure the threads to your work surface using a piece of electrical tape just above the knot. Press the tape firmly over the threads so that the threads do not come lose. A cutting board, laminated tray or piece of cardboard make excellent portable surfaces on which to do your braiding.

3 Some projects will then ask you to braid an extra 2 in length before you start braiding the bracelet. Keep an even pressure on the threads when braiding so that they remain straight. Secure the end of the braided section to your work surface with electrical tape. Press the tape firmly over the braid.

Finishing off

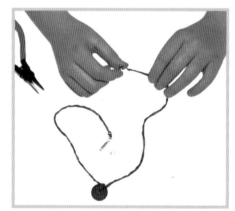

To finish a bracelet—divide the threads at the end of the braid into three even groups and braid together. This braid should be the same length as the one at the other end of the bracelet. Tie a knot at the end of the braid before threading on beads. Keep the beads in place with another tight knot. Trim the threads.

To finish a necklace—tie a tight knot at the end of the braid. Use pliers to close a jewelry clamp over the knots at both ends of the braid. Open the metal rings using pliers and attach a metal ring to each clamp. Separate the sections of the jewelry fastener and attach one section to each ring. Close the rings.

To finish a headband—tie a tight knot close to the end of the braid and thread beads on. You can thread beads onto each thread or use a large bead through which all the threads will pass. To hold the beads in place, tie another knot. The knot must be large enough to keep the bead from falling off.

Tying off

Tying on a bracelet—ask a friend to help tie a double knot. If there is no one around to help, you could tie the bracelet around your ankle instead.

Fastening a necklace—place the necklace around your neck with the opened fasteners at the front. To line up the clasps, look in a mirror.

Tying on a headband—if you cannot do it yourself, ask a friend to tie the ends in a double knot or in a bow at the back of your head.

Braiding tips

The first thing you must do before starting a friendship bracelet design is to read carefully through the instructions and look at the photographs. The second thing to do is to make sure you have the right thread and have carefully measured out the lengths needed. Double-check that you have the right number of threads in the right colors.

If you are doing a complicated design it can help to use the same colored threads as used in the project. Then, when you have mastered that braiding technique, you can go on to make the bracelet, necklace or anklet using your own wonderful color combinations.

To give your bracelets a professional look, try to keep the tension on the threads even. An uneven tension will make the bracelet twist and buckle.

Using your imagination

The colors and beading ideas used in these projects are just to get you started. There is really no end to the sorts of things you can do to make your friendship bracelets unique. Here are some ideas that you might like to try.

❖ Tightly knot together leftover lengths of thread and trim excess threads. When you braid with these multicolored threads you will create a bracelet of many colors. These lengths of thread are also useful when trying out a new braiding technique.

❖ Beads with very small holes, buttons and sequins can be sewn onto a completed bracelet using ordinary sewing needle and sewing thread.

❖ Use textured or glittery threads in your designs.

Looking after your materials

❖ To keep your leftover threads in order, wind them around rectangles of thick cardboard. To keep them from unraveling, insert the thread ends into a small slot cut into one edge of the cardboard.

❖ To keep your scissors sharp, do not use them to cut paper.

❖ Store your beads and jewelry equipment in closed containers. This will keep you from losing them and, more importantly, will keep them out of reach of young children.

Twisty Bracelet

This bracelet is almost like mixing a palette of colored paints. But instead of using paints, you are twisting threads together to make new colors.

YOU WILL NEED THESE MATERIALS

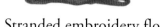

Stranded embroidery floss

Electrical tape   Scissors

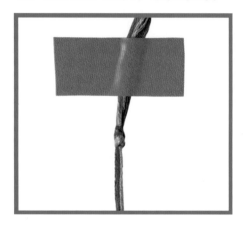

1 You will need six threads of different colors, each 27 in long. Tie them in a knot, 4 in from the top of the threads. Fasten them to your work surface with electrical tape just above the knot.

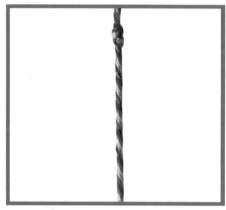

2 Hold the ends of the threads together and twist them together in the same direction until they feel tight. The threads will start to get shorter.

3 Pull the twisted length straight and place your finger in the center of it. Fold the twisted length in half and carefully remove your finger. As you do this, the twisted threads will wind around each other.

Handy hint

Be sure to hold on tightly to the twisted braid. If you let go before you have secured it with a knot, the twist will unwind.

4 Remove the electrical tape and tie a knot in the free end. Tie this knot as close to the end as possible. Trim any uneven threads with your scissors. To fasten the bracelet around your wrist or ankle, push the knot through the loop at the other end.

Hippy Headband

Dress up as a happy hippy and wear this colorful band around your head. The more threads you use, the wider the braid will be. Why not make a bracelet to match?

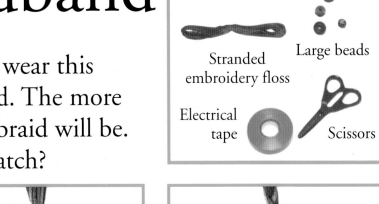

YOU WILL NEED THESE MATERIALS

Stranded embroidery floss

Large beads

Electrical tape

Scissors

1 Cut 12 lengths of thread, each 5 ft long. Tie them in a knot 6 in from the top of the threads and fasten them to your work surface with a piece of electrical tape just above the knot.

2 Divide the threads into three groups, each with four threads. Continue braiding the threads until the band is long enough to fit around your head. Try to keep the tension on the threads even or the braid will twist.

3 Tie the threads at the end of the braid in a knot. Remove the tape.

4 Thread beads onto both ends of the headband and secure with knots. Thread another bead onto each end and tie another knot. Trim any uneven threads. To make a bracelet to match, cut 12 threads, each 16 in long. Then follow steps 1 to 4.

To make it easy to thread the beads onto your headband, wrap a little tape around the end of the threads. This will keep the threads together and keep them from fraying.

Jungle Bracelet

This bracelet is inspired by the colors you would see on an African safari. So when choosing your threads, look for brown, ocher and yellow. You could choose your own theme, such as a rainbow, a sunset or a season, and select colors to coordinate with that theme.

YOU WILL NEED THESE MATERIALS

Stranded embroidery floss

Electrical tape

Scissors

Decorative beads

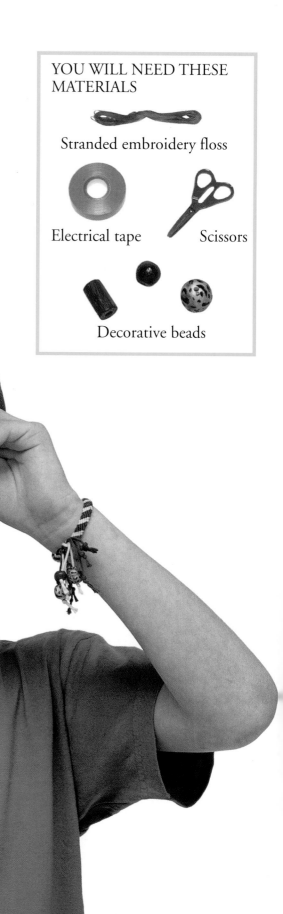

1 Cut three threads of one color and two of another, each 40 in long. Tie the threads in a knot, 6 in from the top. Fasten the threads to the work surface with electrical tape just above the knot. Lay out the threads, as shown.

2 Start with the thread on the far left (in this project it is a brown thread). Take this thread over the orange thread on the right, back under the orange thread, through the loop and over itself. Pull gently to make a knot and repeat.

3 Continue the same knotting technique as shown in step 2, making two knots on each of the remaining threads on the right, until you get to the end of the first row. The brown thread will finish on the right.

4 Take the new thread on the far left (an orange thread) and make a new row of knots as shown in steps 2 and 3.

5 Continue knotting the bracelet until it is the right length to fit around your wrist or ankle. Tie the threads in a knot to secure the braid.

Easy way to learn

If you have never made friendship bracelets before it may help if you use the same color threads as used in the photographs. This will make it much easier for you to follow the steps and use the correct threads. When you have mastered a braiding technique, then you can go on to create one using your favorite colors.

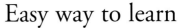

6 Braid the loose threads for 2 in and tie the end of the braid in a knot. Thread a bead onto each thread. Secure each bead with a knot.

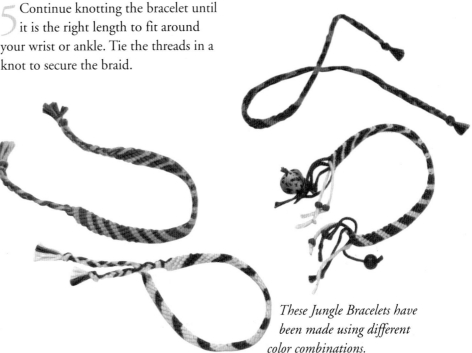

These Jungle Bracelets have been made using different color combinations.

15

Woven Bracelet

This popular style of friendship bracelet uses a very easy weaving technique. If you want to make a really wide bracelet, weave two bracelets and then sew them together using standard embroidery floss and a needle.

YOU WILL NEED THESE MATERIALS

Cotton knitting yarn

Electrical tape   Scissors

Woven Bracelets look really good in strong, bold colors like red and yellow, purple and blue or even black and white. When weaving this bracelet, hold the threads tightly, otherwise the threads will unwind and you will have to start all over again!

1 Cut two threads in one color and two in another, each 31 in long. Fold them in half and tie the ends by the fold in a knot, 2 in from the top. Fasten the threads to your work surface with electrical tape close to the knot. Arrange the threads in color pairs.

2 Start with the far right pair of threads (in this project they are blue) and take them under the blue pair and purple pair next to them, then back over the purple pair. Leave them in the middle, as shown.

3 Take the pair of purple threads on the far left that you have not used yet. Take these threads under the purple and blue pairs next to them, then back over the blue pair. Leave the purple pair in the middle.

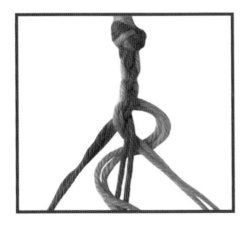

4 Pull the pairs of threads up tightly to the top. Then go back to the blue pair of threads on the far right and repeat steps 2 and 3 until the bracelet is long enough to fit around your wrist.

5 Tie the threads in a knot at the end of the weaving. Snip the looped threads at the top of the braid. You can leave the ends as they are or braid them.

Woven belt

If you have lots of patience and lots of chunky cotton yarn, you can make a woven belt. Take your waist measurement and cut lengths of yarn that are three times the size of your waist measurement. If you want long lengths of loose threads at the ends, cut them a little longer. Make your woven belt following the instructions for Woven Bracelet.

Funky Bracelet

This chunky bracelet uses ten strands of knitting yarn. You have to hold the threads firmly, or the weaving will be uneven.

YOU WILL NEED THESE MATERIALS

Cotton knitting yarn

Electrical tape   Scissors

1 Cut five different colored threads, each 32 in long. Fold the threads in half and tie in a knot, 2 in from the fold. Fasten the threads to your work surface with electrical tape above the knot. Lay the threads out, as shown.

2 Start with the far right pair of threads (in this project they are yellow) and weave them over the pink pair, under the blue pair, over the green pair and under the purple pair. Pull the yellow threads up tightly and leave on the left.

3 Take the pink pair and weave them over the blue pair, under the green pair, over the purple pair and under the yellow pair. Pull the pink threads up tightly and leave on the left.

4 Repeat steps 2 and 3 with each new pair of threads on the far right, until the braid is the right length. Tie the end in a knot and cut the top loop.

To make a Funky Bracelet or anklet for a special occasion, you could replace two colored threads with glittery gold and silver threads.

Star Pin

This glitzy pin gleams with shiny beads. Why not make a pair of earrings to match it? The earrings are just as easy to make as the pin, but do not forget to make two!

YOU WILL NEED THESE MATERIALS

Pencil
Rolling pin
Beads
Paintbrush
Self-hardening clay
Cardboard
White glue
Felt
Modeling tool
Jewelry pin

1 Draw a large star and two smaller ones on cardboard. Cut them out. Roll out some clay ⅛ in thick. Place the stars on the clay and cut around them.

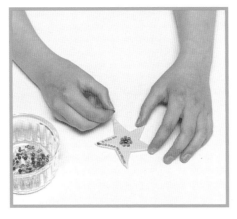

2 Make a pattern of beads on the clay stars. Press them a little bit into the clay to stop them from coming loose.

3 Paint glue over the beaded stars. This will help seal the beads in the clay and give the stars a smooth finish. Set the stars in a warm place to dry. The clay will harden in about 24 hours.

4 Place the templates on felt, draw around them and cut out. Glue the felt stars to the back of the pin and earrings. Glue the jewelry pin and clip-on earring attachments to the felt.

You could try making different shaped sets of matching pins and earrings. How about hearts or circles?

19

Stripes Galore Bracelet

This is one of the most popular styles of friendship bracelet and, if you are a beginner, it is a good one to start with. The more threads you have, the wider the bracelet will be. The more colors you use, the brighter it will be.

Handy hint

This bracelet consists of wide stripes in three colors, but you can also braid it using six threads of different colors. The stripes will be narrower, but your bracelet will be much more colorful. To make this striped bracelet, choose six threads of contrasting colors and follow the instructions in steps 1 to 6.

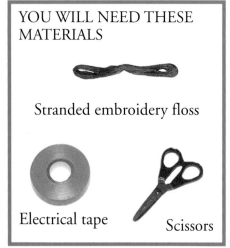

YOU WILL NEED THESE MATERIALS

Stranded embroidery floss

Electrical tape   Scissors

1 Cut six threads, two of each color and each 40 in long. Knot them together, 4 in from the top of the threads. Fasten the threads to your work surface with electrical tape, close to the knot. Lay the threads out, as shown.

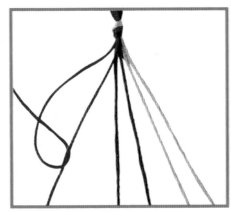

2 Start with the thread on the far left (in this project it is a pink thread). Take the thread over the pink thread next to it, then back under the pink thread, through the loop and over itself. Pull the thread gently to make a knot.

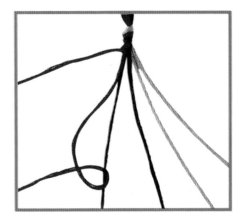

3 Repeat step 2. Still using the same thread, make two knots on the purple thread. Continue to knot the remaining purple and green threads with the pink thread in the same way until you reach the end of the first row.

4 Go back to the new thread on the far left, which is another pink thread, and repeat steps 2 and 3 to make another row. Now the new thread on the far left will be a purple thread. Knot it in the same way.

5 Continue knotting each new far left thread over the other threads to build up stripes of the three different colors. Keep braiding until the bracelet is the right length to fit around your wrist or ankle.

6 Tie the threads at the end of the braid in a knot. Braid the loose threads at both ends of the bracelet for 2 1/2 in and secure the braids with knots. Carefully trim any uneven threads with scissors.

The Stripes Galore Bracelet on the right has been finished with braids. The bracelet on the left has not been braided, therefore leaving long, loose threads.

Stripes and Beads Bracelet

This bracelet has beads threaded into it to add extra sparkle, color and texture. Use small or medium-size beads, but make sure the hole of each bead is large enough for the thread to fit through.

Handy hint

It is a good idea to sort out which beads you are going to use before you start braiding the bracelet. It is hard enough holding onto the right threads without having to fumble around in a jar of beads at the same time.

YOU WILL NEED THESE MATERIALS

Soft embroidery floss

Electrical tape

Scissors

Small and medium beads

1 You will need four threads, each 40 in long. Tie the threads in a knot, 4 in from one end. Fasten them to the work surface with electrical tape above the knot. Lay threads out, as shown.

2 Take the thread on the left (a purple thread) over the pink thread next to it and back under, through the loop and over itself. Pull the thread to make a knot. Repeat to make another knot.

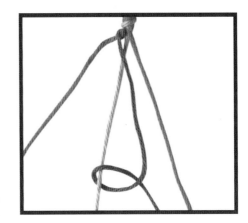

3 Make the same knots on the blue and the orange threads using the purple thread. You will now have finished the first row and the purple thread should be on the right.

4 Go back to the new thread on the left (a pink thread) and thread a bead onto it. Knot the pink thread following steps 2 and 3.

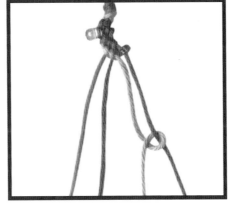

5 Go back to the new color on the left (a blue thread). Knot this thread over the first two threads (orange and purple) and, before you knot it over the pink, thread a bead onto the pink thread and then knot the blue thread over it. This knot will secure the bead.

Fraying threads

The ends of the threads become quite ragged when threaded through beads. To prevent this, wrap a small piece of tape around the ends of each thread before you start braiding.

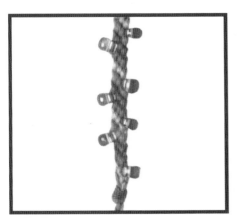

6 Continue to knot and thread on beads until the bracelet is the right length. Tie the threads in a knot.

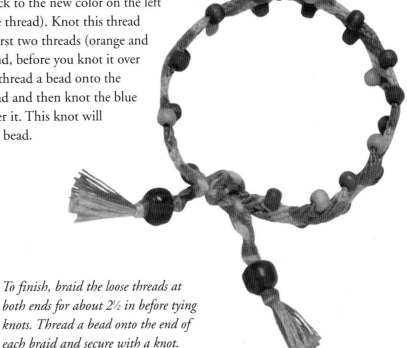

To finish, braid the loose threads at both ends for about 2½ in before tying knots. Thread a bead onto the end of each braid and secure with a knot.

Tic-Tac-Toe

The Tic-Tac-Toe bracelet will really impress
your friends! It looks terrific in black and
white, but could also be braided using the
colors of your favorite football team.

YOU WILL NEED THESE
MATERIALS

Soft
embroidery
floss

Electrical tape   Scissors

1 You will need eight threads in two colors, each 40 in long. Tie the threads in a knot and braid them for 2 in. Fasten the threads to the work surface with electrical tape at the end of the braid. Lay out threads, as shown.

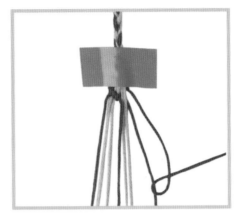

2 Take the thread on the far left (in this project it is purple) and tie two knots on each of the three threads to its right. Leave the purple thread in the middle. Repeat with the purple thread on the far right.

3 Take the purple thread on the middle right and knot it over the middle left thread. Do two knots. Repeat steps 2 and 3 using the three outer pairs of threads. Start with the outermost thread on the left.

4 Knot the far right purple thread over the purple thread next to it. Do two knots. Repeat with far left purple thread.

5 Using the fourth thread from the left, do three knots on each of the threads to its left. Repeat with fourth thread from right.

6 Knot the new middle right thread over the middle left thread, twice. Repeat step 5 to make a cross. Repeat steps 5 and 6 using the purple threads. Knot the middle left pink thread over the thread to its left, twice.

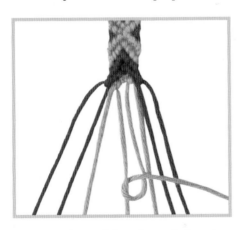

7 Knot the middle right pink thread over the thread to its left, twice. Next, knot the middle right thread over the middle left thread, twice.

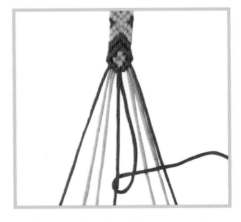

8 To complete the design, repeat from step 2 onward until your bracelet is the right length. To finish, braid 2 in and tie a knot and trim the ends.

Contrasting thread colors, like green and yellow or yellow and purple, makes the tic-tac-toe design stand out.

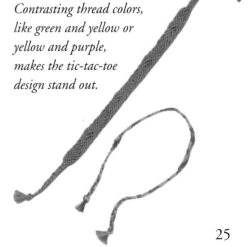

Striped Beaded Barrette

Handy hint

To put dangling beads onto the other end of your braid, carefully undo the knot at the top of the braid. Trim the threads to the same length as those on the other end and then follow the instructions in step 5. Glue the braid to the top of the barrette, making sure that the braid is centered on the barrette.

This barrette really stands out and it is useful, too. It looks great with any hairstyle or length of hair.

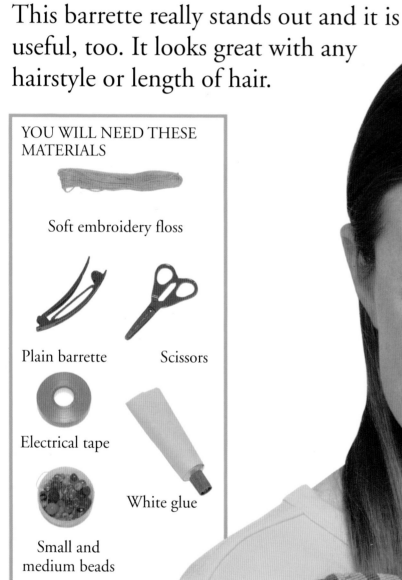

YOU WILL NEED THESE MATERIALS

Soft embroidery floss

Plain barrette   Scissors

Electrical tape

White glue

Small and medium beads

1 Cut ten lengths of thread, two of each color and each 32 in long. Tie the threads in a knot, 6 in from the top. Tape threads to the work surface. Lay threads out, as shown.

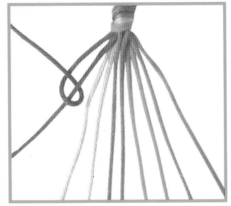

2 Take the dark blue thread on the left over the pale blue thread next to it, back under the thread, through the loop and over itself. Pull the thread gently and repeat the knot.

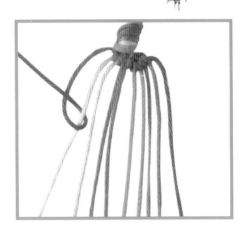

3 Do the same knots on the other threads in the row until the thread you started with is at the end of the row. Go back to the new thread on the far left (another dark blue thread) and repeat the knotting technique explained in steps 2 and 3.

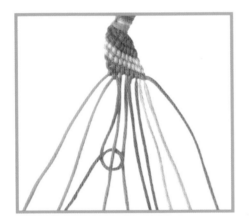

4 Continue knotting the rows with each new far left thread, building up stripes of different colors, until the braid is the same length as the barrette.

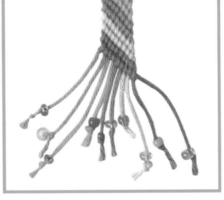

5 Thread small beads onto the end of each thread. Tie a knot on each thread to keep the beads from falling off.

6 Apply glue to the back of the braid and stick it to the top of the barrette Fold the knotted end of the braid to the underside of the barrette and glue.

Knotty Dotty Necklace

Choose lots of your favorite beads to knot into this colorful necklace, or select one really beautiful big bead to knot halfway along the necklace. If you do not have a jewelry fastener to secure your necklace around your neck, tie the ends in a knot.

Handy hint

Before you start braiding, check that the holes in the beads are large enough for the thread to pass through. Craft and hobby stores sell beads made especially for braiding.

YOU WILL NEED THESE MATERIALS

Stranded embroidery floss

Pliers

Scissors

Electrical tape

Jewelry fastener

2 metal rings

2 jewelry clamps

Small and medium beads

1 Cut four threads, two of each color and each 5 ft long. Knot the threads 4 in from the top. Tape them to the work surface above the knot. Lay the threads out, as shown.

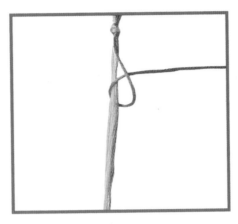

2 Start with the thread that is out on its own (a blue thread). Take it over the other threads, then under them and through the loop. Pull this thread up tightly while holding the other threads.

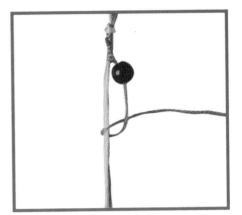

3 After you have knotted a row of about five knots, thread a bead onto the blue thread and then continue to make a few more knots. It is now time to start working with a new thread.

4 Make a new row of knots with the new thread. After five knots, thread on a bead.

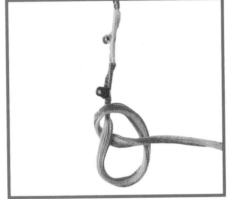

5 Continue making rows of knots and adding beads in this way until the necklace is the length you want. Tie all the threads together in a knot.

Long necklace

You can also make a longer version of the Knotty Dotty Necklace by simply doubling or even tripling the length of the yarns. Do not forget that you will also need lots more beads to decorate your necklace.

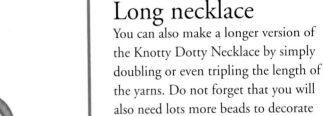

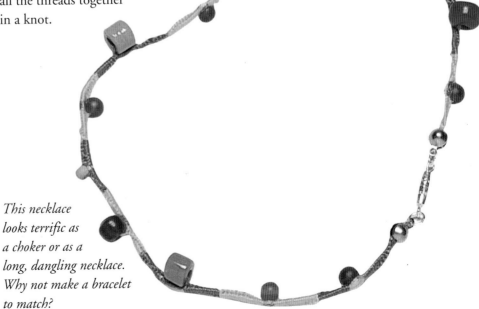

6 Trim the threads close to the knot at each end. Attach a jewelry clamp over each knot and a metal ring to each clamp. Then attach half the jewelry fastener to each of the metal rings.

This necklace looks terrific as a choker or as a long, dangling necklace. Why not make a bracelet to match?

29

Sunglasses Strap

This Sunglasses Strap is very useful and a lot of fun to wear. When you do not want to wear your sunglasses, you can hang them around your neck. You could make Sunglasses Straps for all the members of your family or as gifts for friends.

Handy hint

Some types of jewelry clamps and rings are made of very tough metal. It may be necessary to ask an adult to help you open and close these pieces of equipment using a pair of needle-nosed pliers or jewelry pliers.

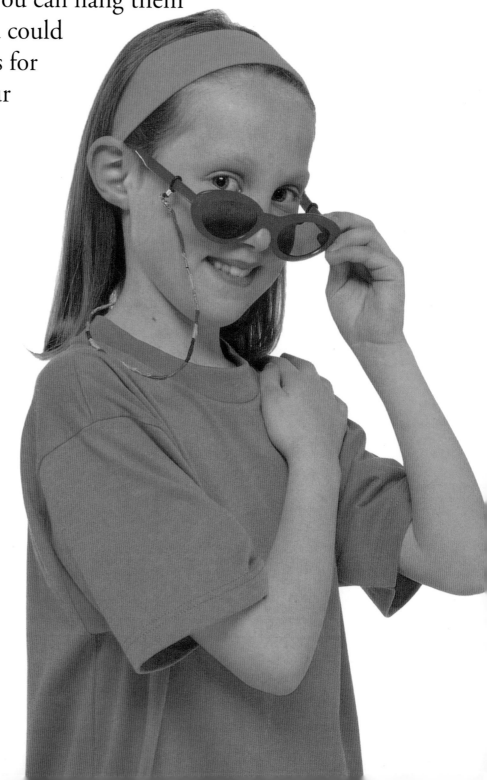

YOU WILL NEED THESE MATERIALS

Stranded embroidery floss

Electrical tape

Scissors

2 metal rings

2 rubber sunglasses attachments

2 jewelry clamps

Pliers

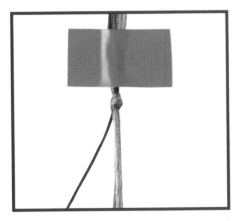

1 Cut six strands of thread, each 6½ ft long. Knot the threads together, 2 in from the top. Tape them to the work surface.

2 Take the red thread that is out on its own and put it over the other threads, then under them and through the loop. Pull the thread up tightly.

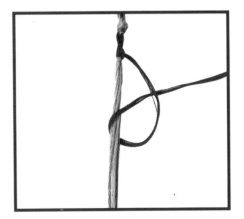

3 Continue knotting this single thread over the others until you have as much as you want of that color and want to change it.

4 Take a new thread and place the red thread with the others. Make a row of knots as shown in step 2. Continue knotting in this way and changing the thread color as often as you wish.

5 When the knotted cord is about 28 in long, tie the threads in a tight knot close to the braid. Trim the loose threads very close to the knot at each end. Take care that you do not cut into the knots themselves.

Using other styles of braid

Many of the other braiding techniques shown can also be used to make the Sunglasses Strap. Whichever Friendship Bracelet design you choose, allow at least 6½ ft of each thread. If you choose to make a wide strap, you may need to use larger jewelry clamps and metal rings.

6 Attach a jewelry clamp over each knot and close the clamps. Attach a metal ring to each clamp and a rubber loop to each ring.

To attach the strap, thread the rubber loops over the arms of your sunglasses and tighten the loops around the arms.

31

Boxes and Bands Bracelet

This is quite a difficult bracelet to make. If you are not pleased with your first attempt, keep practicing until you become an expert.

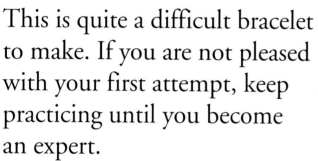

YOU WILL NEED THESE MATERIALS

Soft embroidery floss

Electrical tape

Scissors

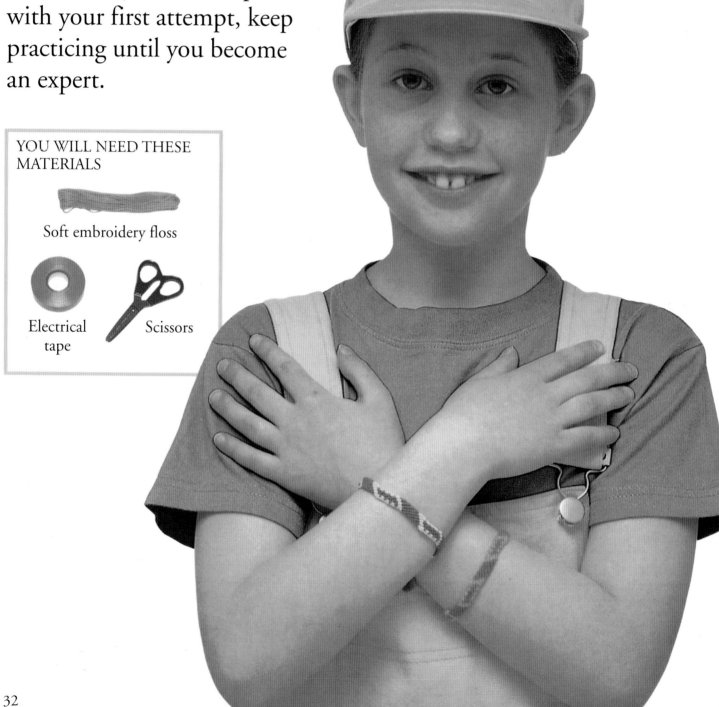

1 Cut two threads in one color and four in another color, each 40 in long. Knot threads and braid for 2 in. Tape threads to work surface.

2 Arrange threads as shown in step 1. Knot the far left thread (dark blue) over the threads to the right. Do two knots on each thread.

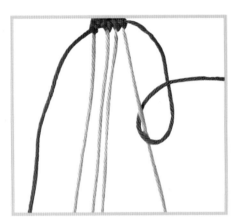

3 Knot the far left thread (also dark blue) over the pale blue thread and do two knots. Repeat, knotting the far right thread over the thread to the left.

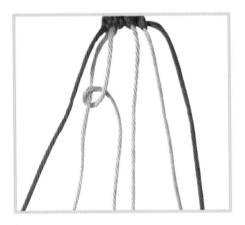

4 Knot the pale blue thread (second on the left) over the thread to the right. Do two knots. Then do one knot over each of the other pale blue threads.

5 Repeat steps 3 and 4 until you have woven four rows of pale blue threads inside a box of dark blue threads. Take care to braid the right thread each time.

6 Take the dark blue thread on the left and knot it over the pale blue thread next to it. Do two knots and return the thread to the starting position. Do the same with the dark blue thread on the far right.

7 Knot the far left dark blue thread over all the threads on the right. Now knot the far left pale blue thread over all the threads on the right until you get to the end of the row.

8 Continue knotting the far left thread over the other threads until there is a dark blue thread on either side of the pale blue threads. Repeat steps 2 to 8 until the bracelet is the right length.

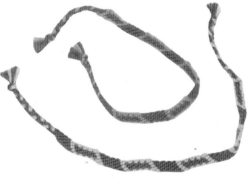

To finish your Boxes and Bands Bracelet, braid 2 in and then tie the threads into a knot. Trim the threads at both ends to the same length.

Arrow Bracelet

You can make the Arrow Bracelet using two, three or four different colored threads. Choose colors to match your best outfit or, if you are making this for a friend, choose his or her favorite colors. To make a thicker Arrow Bracelet, use more threads.

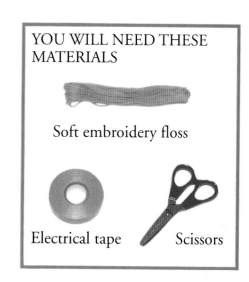

YOU WILL NEED THESE MATERIALS

Soft embroidery floss

Electrical tape

Scissors

1 Cut eight pieces of thread, four of each color and each 40 in long. Knot the threads 2 in from the top and then braid for 2 in. Tape threads to your work surface. Lay the threads out, as shown.

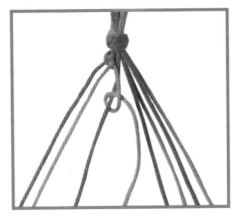

2 Start with the thread on the far left (in this project it is orange) and do two knots on each of the three threads next to it on the right. Leave the orange thread in the middle.

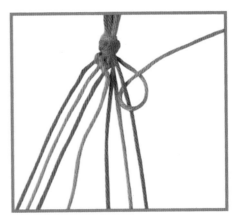

3 Now take the orange thread on the far right and do two knots on each of the three threads next to it on the left. Leave the orange thread in the middle.

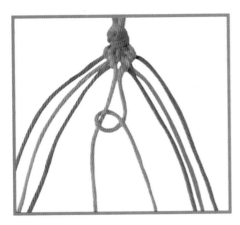

4 Take the middle right orange thread and make two knots over the orange thread on the left.

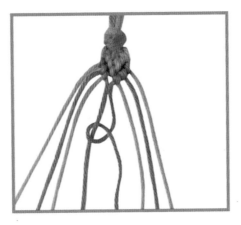

5 Repeat steps 2, 3 and 4, knotting blue and orange alternately until the bracelet is the right length.

6 Braid the threads for 2 in and secure with a knot. Trim any uneven threads with scissors.

Give your Arrow Bracelet a finishing touch by threading large beads onto both ends. Make sure that the hole in the beads will allow eight threads to pass through.

Special Scrunchie

This beautiful hair accessory will make your ponytail very eye-catching. Why not make it in the same color as your favorite outfit or headband? For a special occasion, make a Special Scrunchie from black velvet fabric and shiny metallic beads in gold or silver.

Handy hint

You can also wear your Special Scrunchie as a bracelet or make a pair of matching scrunchies and use them for two ponytails.

YOU WILL NEED THESE MATERIALS

Fabric

Scissors

Tiny and small beads

Sewing needle and, if available, beading needle

Sewing thread

½ in wide elastic

Safety pin

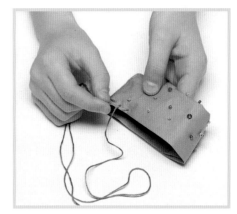

1 Cut a piece of fabric into a rectangle 12 in x 4$^{1}/_{2}$ in. Fold each long side of the fabric over to the wrong side by $^{1}/_{2}$ in. Ask an adult to iron them flat. Sew a selection of beads onto the right side of the fabric, 1 in in from the edges.

2 Fold the fabric (with the beads on the inside) in half lengthwise. Next, stitch the two short edges together, leaving a gap of $^{1}/_{2}$ in in the center of the edge you have stitched. This gap is for the elastic. Now turn the fabric right side out.

3 With the fabric right side out, the beads will be on the outside. Next, fold the fabric horizontally so that the two ironed seams join each other, as shown above. Carefully sew around the edge using thread that is the same color as the fabric you have chosen.

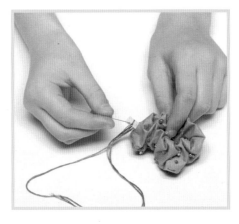

4 To make the fabric scrunch up, cut a length of elastic 16 in long and fasten a safety pin to one end. Thread the safety pin and elastic through the gap and feed it all the way around until it comes back to the gap.

5 Pull the safety pin out of the gap and unclip it from the elastic. Pull the elastic gently to make the fabric ruffle. Tie the elastic in a knot or sew the elastic together to secure it. Trim any excess elastic.

6 Sew up the gap with a small slip stitch. (You may need to ask an adult to show you how to do this stitch.) It is important, especially for this step, that the sewing thread is the same color as the fabric.

Craft tip

If you don't have a beading needle, you can use an ordinary needle instead. Also, to stop the beads from coming loose, use a double thickness of sewing thread and sew each bead twice. Tie a knot when you have finished sewing.

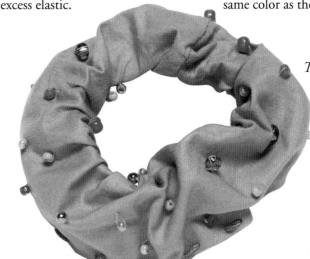

Try making more scrunchies with different kinds of fabric. Which materials work best?

Flower Power

This stylish little Flower Power pin is sure to add a splash of color to a plain T-shirt, sweater, hat or backpack. The choice of colors is all yours. Do not be surprised when all your friends want one too!

YOU WILL NEED THESE MATERIALS AND TOOLS

Pencil

Scissors

Cardboard

Felt

White glue

Sewing thread
Sewing needle

Tiny and small beads

Jewelry pin

1 Draw and cut out a cardboard circle for the flower center and a petal shape. Draw around the circle twice on felt. Cut out. Draw and cut out 16 petals.

2 Sew the beads onto one of the felt circles. Use lots of beads to cover the felt or use just a few in a simple pattern.

3 Turn the beaded circle over and glue the petals all around the edge, as shown. Apply more glue and stick on the second layer of petals, overlapping the first.

4 On the other circle of felt, glue or sew on the jewelry pin and then stick this circle onto the back of the flower. Let the glue dry before trying on your Flower Power pin.

You can go really wild with color combinations for Flower Power pins. Try experimenting to see which colors work best. Do similar colors work or do clashing colors look better?

Hair Wrap

These braids look great! Take it in turns with a friend to do each other's hair. Finish the braid with two beads tied onto the end.

1 Cut three lengths of different colored thread, twice the length of the hair you are braiding. Take a $1/2$-in section of hair and knot the center of the threads around the hair, close to the scalp.

2 Hold the section of hair away from the head. Select one of the colored threads and start winding it tightly around the hair and the other threads. The loops of thread should lie very close together.

3 When you have wound as much as you want of the first color, start winding a thread of another color in the same way. Keep alternating the colors until you reach the end of the hair.

4 To finish, thread a few beads onto the end of the hair and tie a knot in the thread to keep the beads from falling off. Knot the threads around the hair to keep the wrap from unraveling. When you want to remove the wrap, cut off the knot and beads at the end of the wrap and unwind the threads.

Fabulous Hairstyles

Jacki Wadeson

Introduction

Doing your hair is so much fun, and you will be surprised to see how easy it is to create different styles. There are lots of things you can do whether your hair is straight, wavy or curly, short or long. All you need is a brush and comb, and as many brightly colored ribbons, beads, bows, covered bands and fancy barrettes as you can find.

Getting started

First, assemble all the materials and accessories you will need. Then find somewhere to set up your hair salon. Ideally you need a table, chair and large mirror. Ask for permission before you start rearranging furniture and also ask an adult to help set up a mirror, if necessary.

It is also a good idea to ask a friend to join you. A friend can not only do the braids and ponytails at the back of your head, your friend can also tell you just how wonderful you look with your new hairstyle. Having your own hair done is only half the fun—the other half is doing someone else's hair!

Basic techniques

Before you start on the exotic hair styles like Crimping Crazy, Wonder Waves and Beaded Braids, it is a good idea to practice the basic techniques. The basic techniques include the Perfect Ponytail, High Ponytail, Bouncy Pigtails and the Simple Braid. When you have mastered these, then even the

This style uses the basic techniques to create a simply spectacular look. The ribbons are the final touch!

most complicated styles will be easy to do.

It is also important that you comb and brush your hair correctly. Tugging and pulling roughly on your hair will only damage it. Brush your hair with a gentle brush to smooth it and to make it easy to style. To remove knots or tangles, use a wide-toothed comb. Separate out the section of tangled hair and start combing from below the tangle and gradually work your way up the section of hair until the tangle disappears. Never try to force a comb through a knot from above—it will tear your hair.

Making a center or side part in your hair is easy with a wide-toothed comb, but making the part straight requires practice. Your hairstyles will look really professional if the part does not wiggle around like a snake.

Everyone's hair is different and some hair types are better suited to some hair styles. To figure out which styles work best for you is simply a matter of trial and error. If you have flyaway hair, for example, cover a bristle brush with a silk scarf and stroke it over the hair. The static electricity that makes hair wispy will magically disappear. To flatten hair that sticks up, wet your hands with water and smooth them over your hair.

Mini braids look great with beads threaded onto the ends.

Materials

Here are the materials and equipment you will need to set up your hair salon. To create the hairstyles, you do not need a hair dryer or any type of hair gel or lotion. If you go on to create other hair designs and need things like a hair dryer or hair gel, always ask an adult for permission.

Beads Braiding beads have a large hole through which a fine braid can be threaded. They come in lots of different colors and can be bought at craft and hobby stores.

Bobby pins These are used to keep a small section of hair in place. They are made of sprung metal and have plastic, rounded tips so that they do not damage your hair or hurt your scalp. They come in different sizes and colors.

Brush You will need a brush with widely spaced soft bristles. The bristles can be made from nylon or a natural fiber. Keep your brush clean by running a comb through it to remove hairs. Some brushes can be washed under running water. It is always best to have your own brush and comb.

Covered bands You need lots of these terrycloth or yarn-covered stretchy bands. Unlike rubber bands, these bands will not damage your hair. They come in different sizes, thicknesses, colors and textures. You can buy inexpensive packages of covered bands at supermarkets, department stores and drugstores.

Headband Use one of these to keep your hair off your face. All headbands are made of flexible plastic, but some are padded with a soft material and covered in pretty finishes such as fabric, cord or ribbon.

Ribbons You really cannot have too many ribbons when styling your hair. Start collecting ribbons of different widths, colors, textures and patterns.

Scrunchie This is a loop of elastic covered by a wide strip of fabric. You can buy assorted colored scrunchies in lots of different sizes.

Soft curler These soft curlers are easy to use and much more comfortable to wear than other types of curlers. You can buy them at department stores and drugstores.

Thick cord To bind a braid you use a thick cord, or cording, that can be bought on rolls or by the yard at craft and fabric stores. Cord without a shiny, smooth finish is the easiest to use as it will not slide off the braid.

Thread To put beads onto braids you will need to use a thick thread like an embroidery floss. Embroidery floss come in lots of colors. There is even a glittery floss.

Wide-toothed comb This comb has large spaces between the teeth and is good for untangling knots. Always rinse the comb after use.

Wide-toothed comb

Small covered band

Thick cord

Beads

Headband

Thread

Large covered band

Scrunchie

Soft curler

Bobby pins

Yarn-covered bands

Ribbon

Brush

Accessories

Hair accessories are used to decorate your hair rather than to create a style. They are the finishing touch to ponytails and braids. Even a simple barrette can turn an ordinary braid into something special.

Drugstores and department stores are full of colorful and beautiful hair accessories. Some are expensive, others are very inexpensive. When choosing a hair accessory, make sure that it is the right one for your hair and for what you want it to do. Some bobby pins, for example, are made for long or thick hair, others for fine or short hair. Always try to select hair accessories that will coordinate with your favorite outfits or with other hair accessories you want to use.

You do not even need to buy special hair accessories; you can design and make your own using all sorts of unusual materials. Pictured below are hair accessories decorated with

uninflated balloons, fabric flowers, tiny ribbon flowers from a fabric store, and varnished candies.

Here are some other unusual materials that you could use when designing and decorating your own unique range of hair accessories: colorful raffia, string, shells, beads, embroidery floss, papier mâché, tiny toys and dolls, crepe paper (but do not get it wet), plastic bags, gift-wrapping ribbon, strips of leftover fabric, and dried beans and pasta.

To start making hair accessories you will need something to decorate (a plastic headband, a plain plastic-backed barrette or bobby pin), white glue and brush, sewing needle and thread, and your imagination. To get you started you could make the Glitzy Headband on the next page.

If you think that creating fabulous hairstyles is lots of fun, wait untill you start making your own hair accessories!

Tortoiseshell barrette

Fabric sunflower attached to a bobby pin

Velvet bow and fancy button bobby pin

Dingly-dangling bobby pin

Bobby pins decorated with a tiny fabric flower and narrow ribbon

Plastic barrette decorated with candies

Stretchy band decorated with balloons

Chiffon fabric scrunchie

Fabric-covered bendy band

Covered stretchy band with piglet

Stretchy narrow band decorated with beads

Fabric rose and nylon netting rosette attached to bobby pins

Glitzy Headband

Create your own designer hair accessory by simply sewing an assortment of brightly colored beads onto a padded headband.

1 Cut out small dots of felt in lots of different colors. Dab a small spot of glue onto the padded headband where you want each dot to be. Stick the felt dots on and let the glue dry.

2 Carefully sew a bead onto the center of each felt dot. Do two or three stitches. Then knot the thread around the bead. Cut the thread as close as possible to the knot. Do the same for all the remaining beads.

3 To make a different style of headband, select a mixture of beads that matches the color of the headband, or create a rainbow effect by sewing your beads in rows of one color. Use sparkly beads and a black headband to make a special-occasion headband.

Perfect Ponytail

A ponytail is one of the easiest styles to do. It keeps hair tidy and prevents it from getting tangled when playing sports or swimming.

YOU WILL NEED

Scrunchie   Brush

1 Brush your hair straight back off your face using long sweeping strokes to make sure there are no knots. Tease any knots out by brushing gently from the bottom.

2 Place the scrunchie around your wrist. Pull your hair together with your hands at the back of your head. Your hair should go over the top of your ears.

Hair care hint

Scrunchies are very good for holding your hair in place because they do not tear or damage the hair. Ordinary rubber bands can tear your hair when they are removed. If you have very silky or fine hair, it may be necessary to hold the hair in place with a small, yarn-covered elastic before finishing with a large, colorful scrunchie.

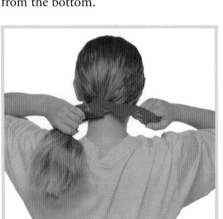

3 Hold your hair in place using the hand on which the scrunchie is wound. Use the other hand to slip the scrunchie off the wrist and over the ponytail. Keep holding the hair while the scrunchie is twisted, as shown.

Thread the ponytail through the scrunchie again (your hands will swap positions). Keep twisting the scrunchie around the ponytail until it is secure.

High Ponytail

A high ponytail, right on the top of your head, makes you instantly taller. This is a cool style that is great for parties and discos.

1 Tip your head forward and brush your hair from the back of your neck right to the ends. Make sure there are no tangles or knots. It is easiest if you use a brush with wide spaces between the bristles.

2 Take hold of your hair with one hand. Run the fingers of your other hand through your hair to make it smooth. Hold your hair and lift your head up.

3 Put a scrunchie over the knuckles of one hand, then pull your hair though the scrunchie. Twist the band and pull your hair through again. Repeat until the scrunchie holds your hair securely.

4 Twist on two more scrunchies above the first one. These will give your ponytail lots of height and make you look really tall. You can use scrunchies in matching or contrasting colors.

To finish, use bobby pins to pin the fabric flowers in place. You can buy fabric or net flowers in the sewing departments of large stores or in fabric stores.

Pony Princess

Here, the top section of your hair is smoothed back into a ponytail halfway down the back of your head. It is then combined with the rest of your hair to make another ponytail.

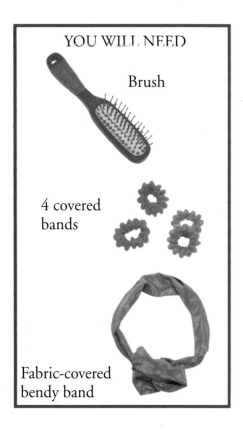

YOU WILL NEED

Brush

4 covered bands

Fabric-covered bendy band

Handy hint

A fabric-covered bendy band is made from a long flexible strip of wire that is sewn into the edge of a strip of fabric. To make the topknot in the band, put the band around your head and then twist the the ends together.

You can wear your Pony Princess ponytail hanging down your back or, if you have very long hair, draped over your shoulder.

1 Brush your hair so that there are no tangles or knots. Then use your thumbs to divide off the top section of your hair, as shown. Hold this section tightly with one hand.

2 Use a covered band to secure this top section of hair. We used terrycloth-covered bands. You may need to twist the band once or twice so that it is tight enough to hold the hair properly.

3 Gather all your hair together at the nape of your neck and secure it in another covered band of a different color. You may need to twist it again so it is tight enough to stay in place.

4 Take another covered band and do the same thing again. The bands should sit neatly next to one another, so push them together.

To finish, place a fabric-covered bendy band around the back of your head. The band can go over or under the ponytail. Bring the ends of the band to the front of your head. Twist the ends together to make a topknot.

5 Add another covered band about halfway down the ponytail. Brush or comb the end of the ponytail to make it smooth.

49

Topsy-Turvy Ponytail

A topknot is great if you are growing out your bangs because it can catch all those little ends that tend to stick out or fall over your eyes.

Handy hint

Twist the ribbons together for a really unusual headband, and choose colors that match your clothes. To keep the ribbons from slipping, it may be necessary to secure them with small bobby pins placed just behind each ear.

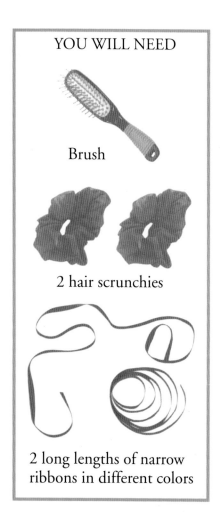

YOU WILL NEED

Brush

2 hair scrunchies

2 long lengths of narrow ribbons in different colors

1 Brush your hair through to remove any tangles or knots. Use the thumb of each hand to divide off the top section of the hair from your ears up to the top of your head.

2 Push a scrunchie or other type of fabric-covered band over the fingers of one hand so that it rests on your knuckles. Clasp the topknot of hair in your other hand.

3 Slip the scrunchie over the hair. Twist the scrunchie and then pull the ponytail through the scrunchie. Repeat until the scrunchie holds the hair securely.

4 Add a second scrunchie and twist it around the top of the first scrunchie. This will give the Topsy-Turvy Ponytail height. If the first scrunchie was large and thick, you may not need to add a second scrunchie.

For an extra-special touch, dress up your topknot by wrapping two long lengths of narrow ribbon around your head like a headband. Secure the ribbons by tying the ends under your hair at the back of your neck. This looks best when the ribbons are different colors.

Bouncy Pigtails

Hair that's at least chin-length can be scooped up into pretty pigtails. Tie them with bright ribbons in fun colors and patterns for school, and add tiny bows for party time.

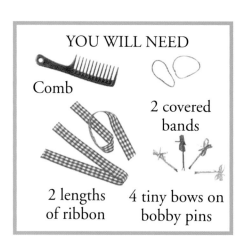

YOU WILL NEED

Comb

2 covered bands

2 lengths of ribbon

4 tiny bows on bobby pins

1 Part your hair in the center from front to back. Put a covered band over one hand, so that it sits on your knuckles. Hold one half of your hair in the other hand.

2 Slip the pigtail through the covered band, holding your hair tightly with one hand. Use your thumb to pull the band tight and then twist it.

3 Put your fingers through the loop in the band and pull the pigtail through. Do this again until the band is tight enough to hold your hair.

4 Tie a short piece of ribbon around the pigtail, then make a bow. Repeat for the other side. To finish, slide two tiny bows on either side of the center part at the front.

Banded Pigtails

Keep your pigtails tidy by wrapping bands of color around them all the way to the bottom. Finish your hairstyle with a pair of decorated bands.

YOU WILL NEED

Comb

Covered bands

Decorated covered bands

1 Part your hair in the center from front to back. Put a plain band over one hand so it sits on your knuckles, then slip it over one section of hair. Twist it back over the pigtail until it is tight. Repeat for the other pigtail.

2 Take two bands (we used ones decorated with piglets) and slip one over each pigtail. You may need to twist the bands twice so that they hold each pigtail tightly.

3 Take two more plain bands and slip a pigtail through each band, about 2 in from the first band. These bands should be a different color from the decorated bands.

4 Take more plain bands (in a different color from the last ones) and add them to your pigtails, always about 2 in from the last band. Continue until you run out of hair or covered bands!

Can you guess what these bands are made from? Lots and lots of small balloons!

53

Be-Bop Pigtails

YOU WILL NEED

Brush

Ribbon

2 covered bands

Comb

High pigtails like these are really easy to do on chin-length or shoulder-length hair. You can twist ribbon around a small section of hair for a really great look!

1 Part your hair in the center and brush your hair so it is really smooth. Take a small section at one side and brush again. Experiment to see how large a section you would like to use.

2 Tie this small section of hair in a covered band. We used crocheted silky bands in a rainbow of colors. You can use your favorite bands but make sure they are not too thick or large.

3 Twist the band and wrap it around the pigtail until it is tight enough to hold the pigtail in place. Repeat for the other side.

Hair care tip

To keep your hair shiny after shampooing, always use cool water for the final rinse.

4 Divide off a small section of the hair from one of the pigtails and slip the end of the ribbon halfway through the covered band. To keep the ribbon in place, tie it onto the band. Twist the ribbon around your hair and tie the ends in a knot and then a bow.

Teeny Bopper

You can use bouncy curls and waves to create lots of styles. The Teeny Bopper style makes it look as though your hair is much thicker than it really is!

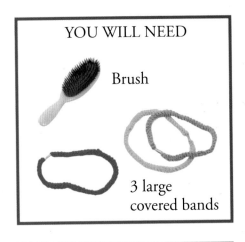

1 Lift a section of hair from the front to the top of your head, and then use a bristle brush to smooth the front of your hair. Do not brush through the length of your hair or you will pull the waves out.

2 Take a large covered band (one that will wrap around lots of times) and use it to secure the top section of hair. Make sure this is right in the middle, because you do not want your topknot to be lopsided.

3 Separate out a section of hair from one side of your head. Fasten it with another large, covered band in a different color. Loosen the waves with your fingers, but do not brush your hair.

4 Do exactly the same with a section of hair on the other side of your head. Do not forget to use a different colored band.

This girl is ready to dance. When she dances, her curls will bounce and bop!

Simple Braid

A three-stranded braid is a lot easier to do than it looks. Braids are really useful for keeping your hair under control, especially when swimming.

YOU WILL NEED

Comb

Brush

2 covered bands

1 Part your hair from center front to the nape of your neck. Divide one half of your hair into three equal sections and hold the back and front outer sections.

2 Cross the back section over the center section. Use your fingers to make sure that the other two sections remain separate. Pull gently on the back section as you cross it over.

3 Cross the front section over the center section. Gently pull all three sections evenly as you work, so that the braid is straight.

To finish, hold your braid 2 in from the end. Take a covered band and slip it over the end, then twist it back over as many times as needed to keep the braid secure.

4 Now you can see how the braid is beginning to form. Continue braiding by crossing the back section over the center section, and the front section over the center section.

Triple Twist

This is a perfect style if your hair is thick and wavy. A ponytail is divided into three sections and each section is braided. Then these braids are braided to make one braid.

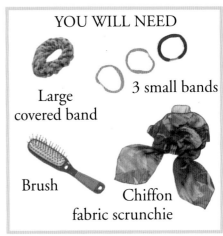

YOU WILL NEED

Large covered band

3 small bands

Brush

Chiffon fabric scrunchie

1 Brush your hair into a low ponytail at the nape of your neck using a wide-bristled brush. Make sure the front and sides are really smooth. Secure the ponytail with the large covered band.

2 Divide the ponytail into three equal sections. Take the first one and braid it from top to bottom. If your hair is long enough, bring the braids over to the front of your shoulder.

3 When you get to the end of the braid, secure it with a small band. Braid the other two sections in exactly the same way. You now have three braids to work with.

4 Take the three single braids and braid them together in the same way as before. Your hair will form into a beautiful thick braid that looks like a twist of hair.

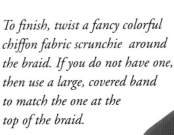

To finish, twist a fancy colorful chiffon fabric scrunchie around the braid. If you do not have one, then use a large, covered band to match the one at the top of the braid.

Pretty Braided Flips

Braids can be bound tightly with cord for a really unusual and striking style.

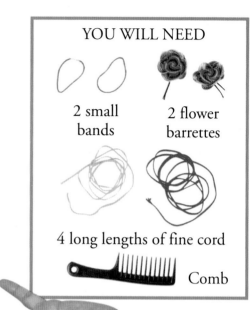

When choosing the cord to bind your braids, avoid those with a very shiny, smooth finish. These cords are difficult to knot and they will slip off the braid.

1 Part your hair in the center, and then braid the hair on one side from the top to the ends. Keep the tension even so that your braid is straight.

2 Secure the end of the braid with a covered band, twisting it back over until it holds the braids tightly. Do the same with the remaining hair.

3 Take a piece of cord and, starting at the top, bind the braid by wrapping the cord tightly around it. Keep the circles of cord close to each other.

Add flowers or matching barrettes to each side of your head, at the front or above the braids.

4 Halfway down the braid, change the color of the cord. Hold the ends of the first and second colors against the braid and bind the new color tightly around the ends. Continue binding until you reach the end of the braid.

5 Secure the end of the cord by tucking it into the covered band that holds the braid together.

Racy Ribbons

Braids look good if you include ribbons as you go. At the ends, tie each ribbon into a bow for a really beautiful cascade of color.

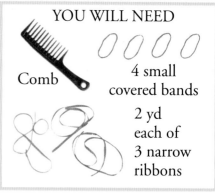

1 Part your hair in the center and brush it through. Gather up the hair at each side and use a covered band to secure in pigtails. Make the pigtails at about ear level. Cut the ribbons in half.

2 Take three lengths of ribbon, each of a different color. Pull the ends halfway through the band, then tie them onto it once. Make sure the ends are even.

3 Divide the hair into three sections and put two matching pieces of ribbon with each one. Braid the hair as usual but include the lengths of ribbon in the braid.

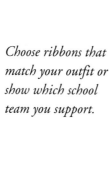

4 Secure the end of the braid, including the ribbons, in a small covered band. Now take each pair of matching ribbons and tie them in a bow. Braid and tie the other side.

Choose ribbons that match your outfit or show which school team you support.

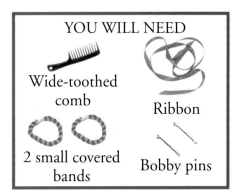

Ribbon Roll

It is easy to make very curly hair look neat and tidy if you braid a high ponytail with ribbon and twirl it into a roll.

YOU WILL NEED

Wide-toothed comb

Ribbon

2 small covered bands

Bobby pins

1 Use a comb with widely spaced teeth to help you smooth your hair up to the top of your head. Hold your hair with one hand and put a small covered band over the other hand. Twist the band around your hair several times to secure the ponytail.

2 Braid the ponytail from the top right down to the ends. Secure the ends with another small covered band. You could leave your hair just like this if you wanted to.

3 Take a length of the ribbon and slip one end under the covered band at the top of your head and pull through, so the ends are even. Bind the ponytail with the ribbon right down to the ends.

4 Take the ends of the ribbon along with the braid in one hand and roll everything around on itself to make a bun. Use one or two bobby pins to secure the bun in place. Allow the ends of the ribbon to dangle free.

The Ribbon Roll looks very classy. It is the perfect hairstyle for a special occasion like a wedding or fancy party.

Beaded Braids

Fine braids with beads threaded through the ends look spectacular. Bead just a few braids around your face or ask a friend to help you do them all over your head.

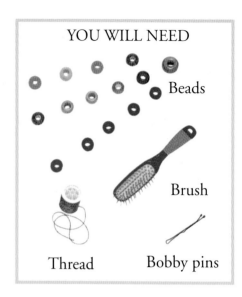

YOU WILL NEED

Beads

Brush

Thread   Bobby pins

Safety!

Make sure you always keep your hair beads in a safe place away from babies or small children, who may think they are candies.

Add colorful beads—as many as you wish—to brighten up your hair.

62

1 Braid a small section of hair down one side of your face. Secure the ends with a bobby pin. Fold a 7-in piece of glittery thread to make a loop.

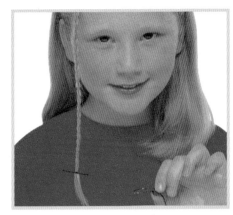

2 Pass the looped end of the glittery thread through the center of the bead. This is easy if the bead has a large hole in the center.

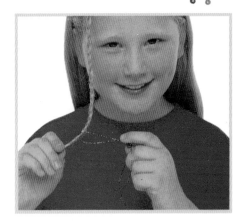

3 Remove the bobby pin and pass the end of the braid through the loop of thread. Make sure you keep a firm hold on the bead, so that it does not fall off.

4 Push the bead toward the braid, then pull on the ends of the thread. This will pull the braid through the hole in the bead. Continue pulling until the end of the braid comes through the bead.

5 Wrap the thread around and around the end of the braid, making sure the strands lie flat. Continue until you have covered 1/2 in of hair below the bead.

Beads galore!

To put more than one bead on each braid, complete up to step 4 and then thread another bead onto the glittery thread. Push the bead towards the braid and then pull on the thread so that the braid comes through the hole in the bead. Repeat as many time as you like before following steps 5 and 6.

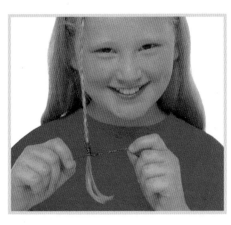

6 Cross over the ends of the thread, then tie a tight knot close to the braid. Trim the threads but be careful not to trim your hair.

Beaded braids look best if the beads on each braid are level.

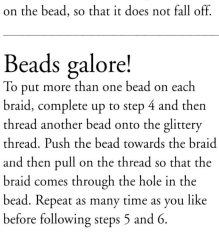

Braids and Bows

Simple braids can be tied at the back of the head in a pretty bow, while tiny front braids can be decorated with small beads.

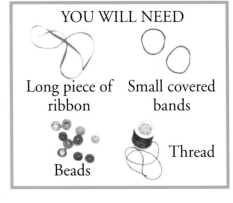

YOU WILL NEED

Long piece of ribbon

Small covered bands

Beads

Thread

1 Part your hair in the center, then take a small section of hair from one side. Start braiding near the roots and work all the way down to the ends. Secure the ends with a covered band.

2 Take a small section of hair from the other side of your head and braid in the same way. Secure the ends in a covered band, twisting and wrapping the band around until it holds tight.

3 Take the braids around to the center of the back of your head. Tie them together with a long piece of ribbon and loop it into a bow. Leave the ribbon ends dangling.

4 Braid two more sections of hair, so that each one hangs in front of an ear. Thread three different-colored beads onto each braid (see Beaded Braids). Try to match some of the beads to the color of the ribbon.

In place of the ribbon bow you can tie back the braids with a fancy scrunchie or decorative covered band.

Bound Braids

Medium-length or long straight hair can be braided, then wrapped with different colored ribbons for a really snazzy style.

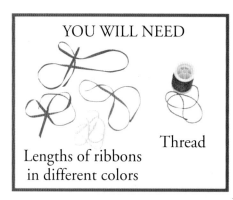
YOU WILL NEED

Lengths of ribbons in different colors

Thread

1 Take small sections of hair and braid them tightly from roots to ends. You will need a friend to help you braid the hair at the back.

2 Secure the end of each braid by winding fine, colorful thread two or three times around each braid. Secure with a firm knot and trim threads.

3 Fold a length of ribbon in half. Tie the ribbon to the top of the braid. The ends should be even. Bind the braid by crossing the lengths of ribbon over and over, first at the front of the braid, then at the back.

Handy hint

For each braid you will need a length of narrow ribbon that is three times the length of the braid.

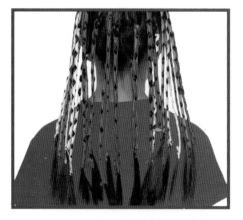

4 Continue binding until you reach the end of the braid. Tie the ends of the ribbon in a tight knot. Repeat until you have bound all your braids. You will need a friend to help you bind the braids at the back of your head.

Crimping Crazy

You do not need a crimping iron gadget to create soft ripples in your hair—all you have to do is braid your hair in lots of fine braids. You will need to leave the braids in overnight to set, so do not leave this fabulous hairstyle to the last minute!

Hair care hint

When unraveling the braids, be gentle and patient. If you pull roughly on your hair you will damage it. Untangle any knots by starting at the hair ends and working upward with a wide-toothed comb.

If you use only a wide-toothed comb on your crimps, they should last until you next wash your hair.

YOU WILL NEED

Wide-toothed comb

Thread

Headband

Fabric flowers

1 Divide your hair into fine sections and braid it from the roots to the ends, making the braids even and quite tight. The smaller the sections are, the finer the finished crimp will be.

2 Secure the end of each braid with a piece of thread, wrap it around two or three times and then tie the ends into a little knot. If you prefer, you can use very small covered bands.

3 Leave the braids in overnight to set your hair into lots of soft ripples. You can lightly mist your hair with water if you wish, but do not go to bed with wet hair.

4 In the morning carefully unravel each braid, loosening it with your fingers as you go.

5 You can leave your hair loose and flowing or keep it off your face with a headband. For a special occasion make two small pigtails at the front and tie on fabric flowers with cord or ribbon.

Wonder Waves

Straight hair can be changed into a mass of waves by using soft curlers. You can leave the curlers in overnight, but even after a few hours you can achieve wonderful results.

Handy hint

You will get tighter and curlier Wonder Waves if your hair is just slightly damp when you put the curlers in. The easiest way to dampen your hair is with a water mist sprayer, but ask for permission before you borrow one. Never go to bed with wet hair.

YOU WILL NEED

Lots of soft curlers

Fabric flower   Brush

To make your lustrous locks look even more wonderful, tie a small ponytail at the top of your head. Secure with a covered band and use a bobby pin to pin a brilliant fabric flower to the front of the ponytail. Fan out the ponytail so that it falls naturally around the sides and back of your head.

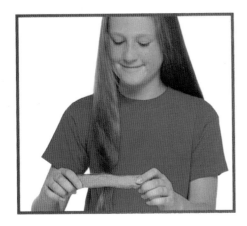

1 Take a soft curler and fold it in half to grip a section of hair between the two pieces. Pull the curler right down to the bottom of the hair.

2 Wind the soft curler up the hair from the ends towards your head. Do this slowly and make sure you do not let go of either end of the curler.

3 When you can wind no further, hold the ends of the curler and bring them together. Cross the ends over to lock the curler in place.

4 Repeat all over your head. Remember, the bigger the sections of hair you wind, the looser the wave will be. For really tight curls, take only small sections and use lots of curlers.

To reveal your Wonder Waves, gently undo and remove each curler. Use your fingers to rake through each wave. You will look amazing!

5 Leave your curlers in overnight. They are very soft, so they are comfortable to sleep in.

Modeling Fun

Petra Boase

Thomasina Smith

Introduction

Modeling is not just about making sculptures of animals and people, it is also about creating useful things like pots and plates. Even jewelry can be made from modeling material and then decorated. In ancient cultures, nearly everything needed for cooking or for serving food was made from clay. The clay was then baked to make it hard.

The ancient Greeks used clay to make beautiful pots, called urns, in which they collected water and stored food. These pots were decorated with patterns or pictures, then painted.

After making a few of the models shown here, why not design some of your own? You can try making all sorts of weird and wonderful designs—from bracelets to picture frames—just use your imagination!

Types of Modeling Materials

For the Sun and Star Pot, you will need a special drying modeling material that hardens without baking. You can buy it at toy, craft or hobby stores. The other projects are made with salt dough. This can be made at home using the recipe on the next page.

Always store your modeling materials in sealed plastic bags or airtight containers. This will keep them clean and ready for future use. Drying modeling material will harden if it is left out in the open air.

Basic Modeling Techniques

❖ To soften modeling material, hold it in your hands. Their warmth will soften it and make it easy to model.
❖ To roll out modeling material, apply even pressure with your hands and use a thick glass to get a smooth surface of the right thickness.
❖ To make snake and sausage shapes, roll the modeling material back and forth between the palms of your hands and fingers. Move your hands along the material to make it even.
❖ To make a round ball, gently roll a piece of modeling material between your flattened palms. Cut the ball in half with a modeling tool or butter knife to make dome shapes.
❖ Be patient and mold the material gently. If you press too firmly, ball shapes will be blobs and snakes will be uneven.
❖ To make a flat circle, roll a piece of modeling material between your palms to make a ball. Place the base of a thick glass on top of the ball and press down firmly.
❖ To make textures, smooth seams or to cut modeling materials, it is best to use a modeling tool. For difficult, detailed work such as adding features to a face, a toothpick is perfect.

Paintbrush

Acrylic paints

Modeling tool

White glue

Self-drying modeling materials

How to Make Salt Dough

For some of the projects you need to make
a batch of salt dough.

1 Weigh or measure the correct
amount of flour and salt. Put the
flour and salt in the bowl. Mix them
together using the wooden spoon.

2 Measure scant 1 cup of water in
a measuring cup and gradually
pour the water over the flour and salt.
Mix well.

3 Pour the oil over the mixture and
mix it in well. When all the oil has
been absorbed, remove the dough from
the bowl and place on a clean surface
that has been sprinkled with flour.

4 Knead the dough with your hands
until it is firm, then put it in a
plastic bag or wrap it in plastic wrap.
Place the dough in the refrigerator for
30 minutes before you use it.

Handy hint

If you do not use
all the salt dough
you have made,
store it in an
airtight container
or a plastic bag and put it in the
refrigerator. When you want to use it
again, simply sprinkle it with flour
and knead it. This will soften the salt
dough and make it easy to work with.

Remember that models made with
salt dough will be fragile, so handle
them with care.

Wiggly Snake Frame

Snakes alive! This fun picture or mirror frame will catch everyone's attention. It is bound to be a great hit. Hiss!

Handy hint

The length of the snakes will vary according to the size of your frame. Do not forget that you will have to make two long and two short snakes for a rectangular picture frame.

YOU WILL NEED THESE MATERIALS AND TOOLS

Salt dough (see recipe)

Modeling tool

Cooling rack

Parchment paper

Baking pan

Picture frame

Fine sandpaper

Oven mitts

Acrylic paints

Paintbrush

Varnish

Felt

White glue

Scissors

74

1 Roll out a piece of salt dough and bend it into a wiggly shape. Roll two small balls of salt dough for the eyes and attach them to one end of the snake. Make three more snakes in exactly the same way.

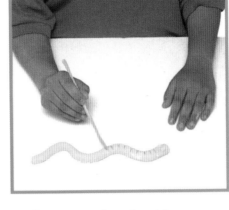

2 Decorate each snake with spots, zigzags or stripes using the modeling tool. Place the snakes on a piece of parchment paper on a baking pan or sheet and bake them for about four hours at 250°F.

3 Ask an adult to remove the hardened snakes from the oven with a pair of oven mitts and to place them on a cooling rack. When cool, lightly rub the snakes with sandpaper before painting and varnishing them.

4 To make a tongue for each snake, use scissors to cut Y-shaped pieces of colored felt. Glue a tongue to the underside of each snake's head. The forked section should protrude from the front of the head.

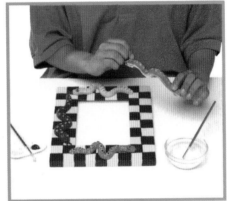

5 Use a pencil and ruler to draw a checkerboard pattern onto the front and sides of the frame. Paint the frame using two colors, as shown. To finish, glue the snakes on, one on each edge of the frame.

Daisy frame

If snakes gives you the shivers, then decorate your frame with salt dough daisies. Follow the steps for Wiggly Snake Frame, but use cookie cutters to make the daisies and the centers.

This cheerful picture frame will add color to any shelf or wall. You could paint the flowers and decorate the frame to match your room. These daisy shapes would look great on round or oval frames, too.

Sun and Star Pot

This pot is made from slabs of modeling clay. The slabs are joined by smoothing the inside seams with a modeling tool. When the pot is complete, smooth the outside seams. This pot is ideal for storing small valuables. To make a nest of pots, make two more pots— one smaller and one larger than your Sun and Star Pot.

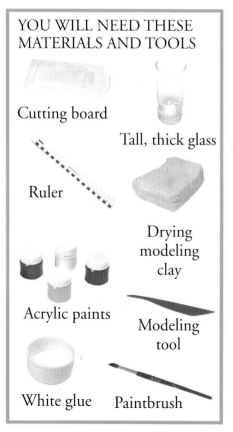

YOU WILL NEED THESE
MATERIALS AND TOOLS

Cutting board

Tall, thick glass

Ruler

Drying
modeling
clay

Acrylic paints

Modeling
tool

White glue   Paintbrush

1 Roll a large slab of clay until it is ¹/₄ in thick. Use an upturned glass to cut out two circles. Cut out two strips, one 10 in x 2 in and one 10 in x ³/₄ in.

2 To make the lid, roll out one of the circles until it is ¹/₄ in wider than the other circle. Score around the side of the lid before pressing on the narrow strip. Bind the edges together.

3 Score the side of the remaining circle and carefully wrap the wider strip of clay around it. Support the sides of the pot as you bind the edges together and smooth the seams.

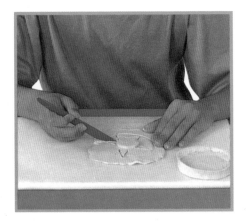

4 Press an upturned glass onto rolled-out clay to make the outline of a circle. Into the center, place a small circle of clay. Carve the sun's rays around it using the modeling tool.

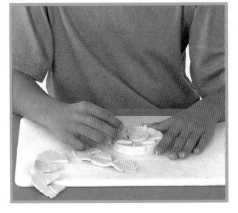

5 Cut out the sun with the modeling tool and position it on the flat, upper surface of the lid. Place the lid on the upturned glass to dry. Allow the pot and lid to dry for 12 hours before turning them over to dry for another 12 hours.

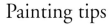

Painting tips

❖ Paint the inside and outside of the pot first. While this is drying, paint the top and the bottom of the lid yellow. Decorate the pot with stars and then go on to complete the lid with the blue and green paint. To finish, paint stars on the lid.

❖ To make the stars and moons really shine, sprinkle gold or silver glitter onto the wet paint.

❖ If you are into astrology, you could paint star signs around the side of the pot or onto the lid.

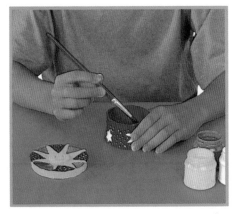

6 Paint and decorate the insides and outsides of the pot and lid. When dry, apply a varnish of 8 parts white glue to 1 part water.

Heart and Star Rings

These rings are great fun and easy to make. To make heart and star templates, draw the shapes onto cardboard and cut them out.

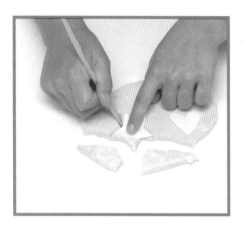

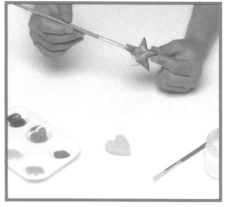

YOU WILL NEED THESE MATERIALS AND TOOLS

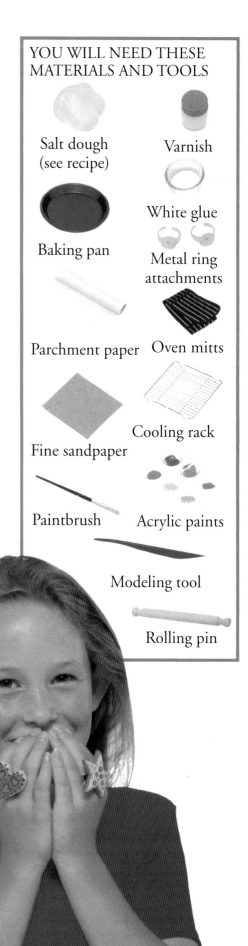

Salt dough (see recipe)

Varnish

Baking pan

White glue

Metal ring attachments

Parchment paper

Oven mitts

Fine sandpaper

Cooling rack

Paintbrush

Acrylic paints

Modeling tool

Rolling pin

1 Roll out a piece of salt dough ½ in thick. Place the heart and star templates on the dough and cut around them with the modeling tool. Place the shapes on a baking pan lined with parchment paper and bake them for about four hours at 250°F.

2 When the shapes have hardened, remove the pan from the oven (using oven mitts) and transfer them to a cooling rack. Once they have cooled, smooth rough edges with sandpaper before painting your rings. When dry, apply a coat of varnish.

3 Glue a ring attachment onto the back of each shape and allow the glue to dry before trying on the rings.

These rings are so easy to make that you will soon be wearing one on each of your fingers!

Heartthrob Bracelet

Dress up for a party and wear this fun bracelet. You could make other bracelets with stars or flowers.

YOU WILL NEED THESE
MATERIALS AND TOOLS

Salt dough (see recipe)

Cardboard

Rolling pin

Cookie cutter

Varnish

Parchment paper

Baking pan

Oven mitts

Cooling rack

Paintbrush

Fine sandpaper

Acrylic paints

Scissors

Glue

1 Roll out a large piece of salt dough to about ¹/₂ in thick. Using a heart-shaped cookie cutter, cut out five hearts. Place the hearts on a baking pan lined with parchment paper and bake them in the oven for about four hours at 250°F.

2 Ask an adult to remove the pan from the oven using oven mitts and to transfer the hardened shapes to the cooling rack. When cool, smooth the edges with sandpaper, then paint the hearts in lots of bright colors. When dry, apply a coat of varnish.

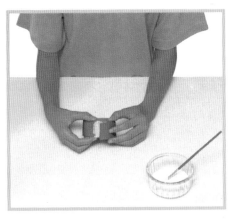

3 Cut a strip of cardboard 8 in x 2 in. Check that it will fit easily over your wrist before gluing the ends.

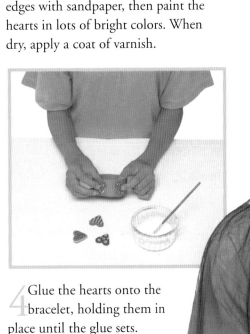

4 Glue the hearts onto the bracelet, holding them in place until the glue sets.

T-shirt
Painting

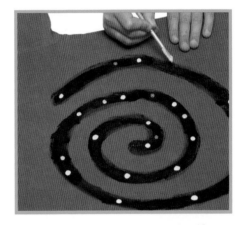

Petra Boase

Introduction

The fluorescent fabric paints on this T-shirt will glow under ultraviolet light.

Decorating T-shirts with fabric paints, glitter and material is fun and very easy to do. In no time at all you will be creating stylish and wacky T-shirts for yourself, friends and family.

This section shows you how to prepare the T-shirts for painting as well as how to use different types of fabric paints to achieve stunning effects. It is also bursting with ideas. There are T-shirt designs for disco dancers and party animals of all kinds. There is even a T-shirt design for the art enthusiast— you could soon be wearing your very own priceless work of art!

These designs could also be used for a costume party or for school plays. All you need to complete the outfits are leggings or shorts, a hat and some make-up.

Most of the projects are simple to do. If you have never done any fabric painting before, it might be a good idea to start on one of the easier projects, such as Swirly Spots, Glitzy Stars or Crazy Spiral.

The colors and types of fabric paints used in the designs are only suggestions. Change them to create different effects and to suit the clothes you will be wearing with the T-shirt. The ultimate design is really up to you. Feel free to modify patterns and to come up with your own ideas.

Safety

❖ Always keep fabric paints and sharp utensils out of the reach of small children.

❖ Read the instructions on fabric paint packaging before you start painting. Follow the manufacturer's guidelines for preparing the T-shirt, mixing and applying paints and for drying wet paint. Some manufacturers will also recommend washing or ironing the painted T-shirt before wearing it.

❖ Ask an adult to iron the T-shirt and to supervise the use of sharp tools.

❖ If you splash fabric paint on your clothes, soak them immediately in lots of cold water. Keep rinsing the garments until the fabric paint is removed. Then wash the clothes in warm, soapy water.

Glitzy Stars would also look great on a dark blue or black T-shirt. This design is simple and quick to do.

This Sea Life Fantasy T-shirt would be great for a day on the beach. The design, which is painted directly on the fabric, will certainly challenge your artistic skills.

Materials and Tools

These are the materials and tools you will need to complete the projects that follow.

Cardboard Large pieces of cardboard are inserted into the body and sleeves of a T-shirt to keep wet fabric paint from seeping through. You can buy sheets of thick cardboard or use cardboard from recycled packaging and boxes.

Chalk fabric marker This is a special white chalk that is used for drawing outlines onto dark-colored T-shirts.

Fabric glitter This is special glitter that can be attached to fabric with fabric glue. It is very fine, so use it carefully.

Fabric glue This glue will stick pieces of fabric together. Always use a special brush for applying fabric glue.

Fabric marker pen A fabric marker pen looks like a normal felt-tip pen, but it is designed to be used on fabric.

Fabric paint Fabric paint is applied to fabric and will not wash out. Read the instructions on the container before using it.

Fluorescent fabric paint Under ultraviolet light, this paint will glow. It comes in many bright colors.

Glitter fabric paint This sparkly fabric paint comes in a tube or squeeze bottle. Always read the instructions on the packaging before using glitter fabric paint.

Hair dryer You will need a hair dryer with a low heat setting to dry puffy fabric paint. Ask permission before using a hair dryer.

Pearlized or iridescent fabric paint This fabric paint dries with a special sheen. It comes in a squeeze bottle.

Puffy fabric paint When dried with a hair dryer, this paint puffs up. It comes in a squeeze bottle. Always follow the manufacturer's instructions when using puffy fabric paint.

Sponge You can buy an inexpensive sponge at a drug store. A sponge dipped in fabric paint and gently pressed onto fabric makes an interesting texture.

Sticky-back Velcro dots These dots stick to each other when pressed together.

T-shirt For the projects you will need cotton T-shirts. There are designs for short-sleeved and long-sleeved styles.

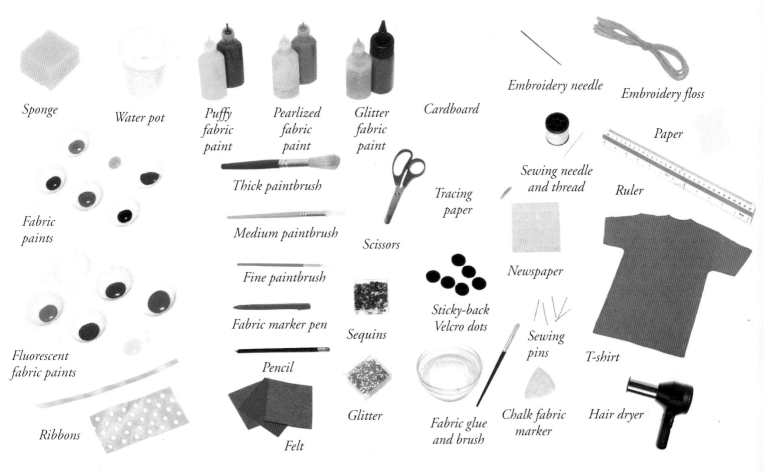

Sponge

Water pot

Puffy fabric paint

Pearlized fabric paint

Glitter fabric paint

Cardboard

Embroidery needle

Embroidery floss

Paper

Thick paintbrush

Sewing needle and thread

Ruler

Fabric paints

Medium paintbrush

Tracing paper

Scissors

Fine paintbrush

Newspaper

Fabric marker pen

Sequins

Sticky-back Velcro dots

Sewing pins

T-shirt

Pencil

Fluorescent fabric paints

Ribbons

Glitter

Felt

Fabric glue and brush

Chalk fabric marker

Hair dryer

Getting Started

Before you can start painting, you must prepare the T-shirt and perfect your design. The more time you spend getting these things right, the more spectacular the results will be.

If you are using a new T-shirt, first wash it to remove excess dye. When the T-shirt is dry, ask an adult to iron it to smooth out creases.

To stop fabric paint from seeping through the T-shirt, insert pieces of cardboard into the body and sleeves. The pieces of cardboard should fit snugly into position.

Draw drafts of your design on a piece of paper before drawing it on the T-shirt. Fabric marker pen, like fabric paint, cannot be washed out.

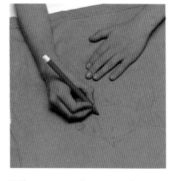

When you are happy with your design, draw it onto the T-shirt. Use a fabric marker pen on light-colored T-shirts, and a chalk marker on dark T-shirts.

When you are ready to start painting and have gathered all the necessary materials and tools, you must cover the work surface with a large sheet of wipe-clean plastic or lots of sheets of newspaper. It is also a good idea to protect any nearby furniture. Fabric paint can splatter, especially if you are flicking a brush loaded with fabric paint to get a special effect. Protect your clothing with an apron and old shirt—fabric paint will not wash off.

Painting tips

Fabric paints come in many wonderful colors and textures, but it is not necessary for you to have everything to create stunning designs on a T-shirt.

Fabric paint colors, just like normal acrylic or poster paint colors, can be mixed to make other colors. This means, for example, that you can mix blue puffy fabric paint with yellow puffy fabric paint to make green puffy fabric paint. You can also mix glitter fabric paint colors to make other colors.

To make fabric paint colors lighter, add white fabric paint to the color or simply add a little water. Fabric paint colors can be made darker by adding a little black fabric paint.

How to mix colors: yellow + blue = green, yellow + red = orange, red + blue = purple.

Mix large batches of a color in a water pot or small bowl. Add a little water to paints to make them go further.

Before painting the T-shirt, try out the techniques and the colors on a piece of leftover fabric. This is especially important when using fabric paints in squeeze bottles.

Puffy paint only puffs up when it is dried with a hair dryer set on low heat. Before drying other fabric paints with a hair dryer, check the instructions on the paint container.

Sunny Sunflower

On the Sunny Sunflower T-shirt you can show off your artistic flair for color, shape and texture. In fact, your painting will be so good that it will be framed in gold. But there is something missing from this painting—the signature of the artist.

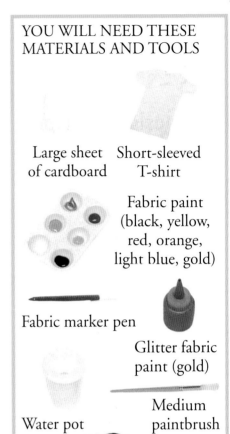
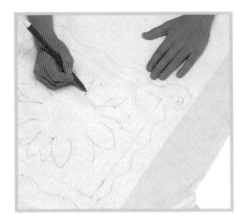

1 Insert a piece of cardboard inside the body of the T-shirt. Use the fabric marker pen to draw the outline of the sunflower and the fancy picture frame.

2 Paint the center of the sunflower with black fabric paint. Use shades of yellow, red and orange to paint the petals. Allow the paint to dry.

3 Use a light blue fabric paint for the background of your sunflower painting. Take care not to paint over the petals or into the frame. Allow the paint to dry.

4 Using a clean brush, paint the picture frame with gold fabric paint. Allow to dry. For the final artistic touch, decorate the gilt frame with swirls of gold glitter fabric paint.

Swirly Spots

The Swirly Spots design is simple to draw and you can use as many colors as you like. The fabric paint must be dry before you decorate the spots with glitter fabric paint.

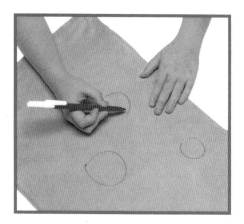

1 Insert pieces of cardboard inside the body and sleeves of the T-shirt. Use the fabric marker pen to draw circles onto the front of the T-shirt. Draw circles onto the sleeves as well.

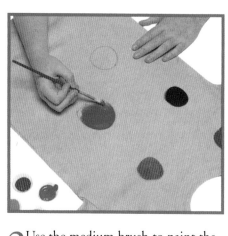

2 Use the medium brush to paint the circles different colors. Do not forget to wash the brush when changing colors. Allow the fabric paint to dry thoroughly before starting the next step.

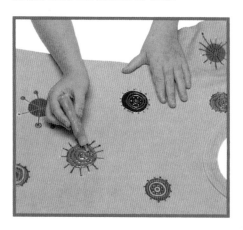

3 Use purple, red, yellow, orange and blue puffy fabric paint to decorate the circles with swirls, lines and dots. Dry the puffy fabric paint with the hair dryer. This will make the puffy paint puff up. To finish, decorate some circles with silver glitter fabric paint.

When using fabric paints in squeeze bottles, keep the nozzle moving smoothly over your design. If the nozzle stays in one place for too long, the paint will form blobs.

86

Glitzy Stars

This twinkling T-shirt is perfect for a party. The glitter and sequins will make the stars sparkle under lights. Special fabric glitter can be bought at hobby and craft stores.

YOU WILL NEED THESE
MATERIALS AND TOOLS

Fabric paint
(blue, yellow,
white, red,
pink, green)

Short-sleeved
T-shirt

Fabric marker
pen

Glitter fabric
paint

Fine paintbrush

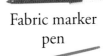

Sequins

Fabric
glitter

Large sheet
of cardboard

Water
pot

Pearlized fabric
paint (yellow)

Fabric glue
and brush

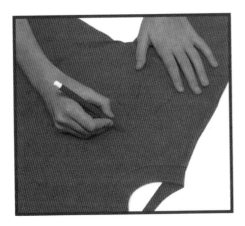

1 Insert a piece of cardboard inside the body of the T-shirt. Use the fabric marker pen to draw the outlines of stars all over the front of the T-shirt. Make some stars large, others small.

2 Use the fine brush to paint the stars with blue, green, red, yellow and pink fabric paints. When dry, paint around the edges of the stars with yellow pearlized fabric paint and gold glitter fabric paint. Decorate the stars with dots of yellow and gold.

3 Now it is time to add some real sparkle to this starry T-shirt. Paint the stars with fabric glue. While the glue is still wet, sprinkle on fabric glitter and sequins. When dry, gently shake the T-shirt over a sheet of newspaper to remove excess glitter and sequins.

If you would like to decorate the back of the T-shirt, wait for the front of the T-shirt to dry before turning the T-shirt over. Check that the cardboard is still in place before repeating steps 1, 2 and 3.

Disco Dazzler

Wear this wild T-shirt to be the center of attention. The patterns will positively glow in the dark under ultraviolet light. This is because they have been painted using fluorescent fabric paint.

YOU WILL NEED THESE MATERIALS AND TOOLS

Short-sleeved black T-shirt

Water pot

Hair dryer

Large sheet of cardboard

Medium paintbrush

Chalk fabric marker

Fluorescent fabric paint (yellow, blue, pink, orange, green)

Puffy fabric paint (orange, yellow, purple, red)

1 Insert pieces of cardboard inside the body and sleeves of the T-shirt. Use the chalk fabric marker to draw the outlines of triangle, spiral and zigzag patterns all over the front and the sleeves of the T-shirt. Draw a zigzag pattern along the bottom edge of the T-shirt.

2 Use fluorescent yellow, blue, pink, orange and green fabric paint to fill in the outlines. To make other colors, simply mix different colors on a palette. Allow the fabric paint to dry before painting patterns onto areas already painted.

3 Decorate the T-shirt with dots and squiggles of orange, yellow, purple and red puffy fabric paint. You can make your patterns as wild as you like. To make the puffy fabric paint puff up, dry it with a hair dryer. Set the hair dryer to its coolest setting.

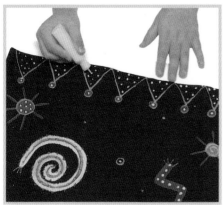

4 Go over the zigzag at the bottom of the T-shirt with orange puffy fabric paint. Use other puffy fabric paints to add circles and dots. Once again, use the hair dryer set to its coolest temperature to dry the puffy fabric paint. Allow your T-shirt to dry thoroughly before hitting the disco and dazzling all your friends.

If you want to continue the zigzag pattern on the back of the T-shirt, wait for the front to dry before turning the T-shirt over. Before starting to paint, check that the cardboard is still in place.

Dazzling colors

Though this design looks great in fluorescent fabric paint colors, it can also be done using brightly colored plain fabric paints. Even though these paints will not glow in the dark, your T-shirt will still be the envy of all at the disco. But if you like a bit of glitz and glitter, why not use glitter fabric paint or fabric glitter?

Sea Life Fantasy

When you look at this T-shirt you can almost smell the salty air, hear the crash of the waves and see the schools of brightly colored fish darting backward and forward in a pale blue ocean. In this design there are only two species of marine life, but you could also add crabs, shells, coral and fronds of seaweed.

This T-shirt design could also be painted onto a long vest or long-sleeved sweatshirt. It would also make a wonderfully relaxing image for a pillowcase.

Handy hint

It is good idea to practice your design for this T-shirt on paper before you start drawing it onto the T-shirt. If you have trouble drawing fish or star shapes, trace them from a book or magazine. The underwater world is a fascinating one, so if you want to get more ideas for painting your T-shirt, look in an encyclopedia or other reference book.

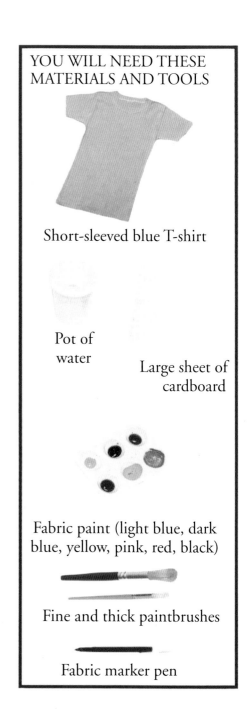

YOU WILL NEED THESE MATERIALS AND TOOLS

Short-sleeved blue T-shirt

Pot of water

Large sheet of cardboard

Fabric paint (light blue, dark blue, yellow, pink, red, black)

Fine and thick paintbrushes

Fabric marker pen

1 Insert the piece of cardboard inside the body of the T-shirt. Use the fabric marker pen to draw the outlines of the fish, starfish and waves onto the front of the T-shirt.

2 Paint the waves with light and dark blue fabric paint using the thick brush. Do not worry if the paint does not go on smoothly—an uneven texture will look more realistic.

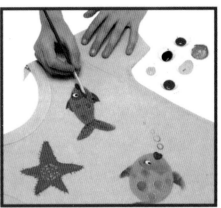

3 Paint the fish in shades of blue, green, pink and red. The green can be made by mixing yellow and blue. Use the fine brush to paint the fish lips and eyes. Paint black bubbles coming from their mouths. Mix red and yellow to make orange. Paint the starfish with the orange paint.

4 Allow the fabric paint to dry. Turn the T-shirt over, making sure that the cardboard is still in position. Use the fabric marker pen to draw another fish onto the back of the T-shirt. Continue the pattern of the waves.

5 Use the thick brush to paint the waves with light and dark blue fabric paint. Wash the brush before painting the fish pink with yellow spots. Paint features onto the fish's face and bubbles coming from its mouth.

Do not forget that this design is called Sea Life Fantasy, so be as creative as you want to be. You could invent exotic creatures to inhabit a fantastic underwater environment.

Crazy Spiral

The Crazy Spiral T-shirt is simple to do, even if you are new to fabric painting. Draw the outline of the spiral as large as you can to make it easy to paint and to decorate. You can add smaller spirals to the design or paint a spiral on the back of your T-shirt, too.

Handy hint

To stop the T-shirt from moving around when you are drawing the outline or painting your design, tape the T-shirt to your work surface with masking tape. Lay the T-shirt out flat, making sure there are no uneven surfaces or bumps, before taping.

YOU WILL NEED THESE
MATERIALS AND TOOLS

Short-sleeved
T-shirt

Large sheet
of cardboard

Fabric
marker pen

Fine, medium
and thick
paintbrushes

Glitter fabric
paint (green,
purple)

Water
pot

Fabric paint
(black, orange,
yellow, light
blue, green)

Pearlized fabric
paint (yellow,
orange, purple)

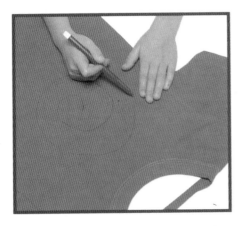

1 Insert pieces of cardboard inside the body and sleeves of the T-shirt. Use the fabric marker pen to draw a large curly spiral on the front of the T-shirt.

2 Paint the spiral with black fabric paint using the thick brush. Allow the paint to dry thoroughly before starting the next step.

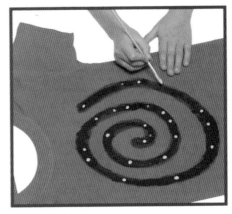

3 Decorate the spiral with orange, yellow, light blue and green dots of fabric paint. Do this using the medium brush. Allow the paint to dry.

4 Draw circles around some of the dots using yellow pearlized fabric paint. Go around the outline of the spiral with orange and purple pearlized fabric paint.

Choosing your own colors

The colors used on this design are suggestions only—you can choose just about any combination of colors you like. You could paint the design using only yellows and oranges, or shades of pink and red. Make sure before you start that your colors will stand out against the color of the T-shirt.

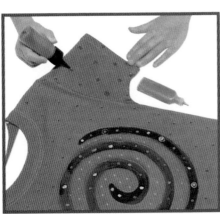

5 Make dots of yellow pearlized fabric paint inside the spiral. Cover the front of the T-shirt with green glitter fabric paint dots. To finish, dot the sleeves with purple glitter fabric paint.

Index

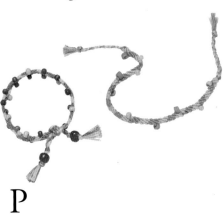

Acknowledgments

The publishers would like to thank the following children for appearing in this book, and of course their parents: Nana Addae, Richard Addae, Mohammed Adil Ali Ahmed, Josie and Lawrence Ainscombe, Clive Allen, Deborah Amoah, Charlie Anderson, Lauren Andrews, Rosie Anness, Michael Apeagyei, Tania Steve Aristizabal, Joshua Ashford, Emily Askew, Rula Awad, Nadia el-Ayadi, Joshua Ayshford, Nichola Barnard, Venetia Barrett, Jason Bear, Michael Bewley, Gurjit Kaur Bilkhu, Vikramjit Singh Bilkhu, Maria Bloodworth, Leah Bone, Catherine Brown, Chris Brown, Christopher Brown, Cerys Brunsdon, William Carabine, Daniel Carlow, Kristina Chase, Chan Chuvinh, Ngan Chuvinh, Alexander Clare, Rebecca Clee, Emma Cotton, Charlie Coulson, Brooke Crane, Charley Crittenden, Lawrence Defraitus, Dean Denning, Vicky Dummigan, Kimberley Durrance, Holly Everett, Alaba Fashina, Benjamin Ferguson, Terri Ferguson, Aimee Fermor, Kirsty and Rebecca Fraser, Fiona Fulton, Nicola Game, George Georgiev, Alice Granville, Lana Green, Liam and Lorenzo Green, Sophia Groome, Alexandra and Oliver Hall, Reece Harle, Laura Harris-Stewart, Jonathan Headon, Dominic Henry, Edward and Thomas Hogarth, Lauren Celeste Hooper, Mitzi Johanna Hooper, Sasha Howarth, Briony Irwin, Kayode Irwin, Gerald Ishiekwene, Saadia Jacobs, Stella-Rae James, Isha Janneh, Jade Jeffries, Aribibia Johnson, Rean Johnson, Reece Johnson, Carl Keating, Karina Kelly, Sarah Kenna, Camille Kenny-Ryder, Lee Knight, Nicola Kreinczes, Kevin Lake, Victoria Lebedeva, Barry Lee, Kirsty Lee, Isaac John Lewis, Nicholas Lie, Sophie, Alex and Otis Lindblom-Smith, Chloe Lipton, Scott Longstaff, Ephram Lovemore, Claire McCarthy, Erin McCarthy, Jock Maitland, Gabriella and Izabella Malewska, Ilaira and Joshua Mallalieu, Elouisa Markham, Alexander Martin-Simons, Laura Masters, Hou Mau, Trevor Meechan, Mickey Melaku, Imran Miah, Yew-Hong Mo, Kerry Morgan, Jessica and Alice Moxley, Aiden Mulcahy, Fiona Mulcahy, Tania Murphy, Moriam Mustapha, Lucy Nightingale, Ify Obi, Adenike Odeleye, Wura Odurinde, Laurence Ody, Folake Ogundeyin, Abayomi Ojo, Fola Oladimeji, Ola Olawe, Lucy Oliver, Michael Oloyede, Yemisi Omolewa, Tope Oni, Alexander and Dominic Paneth, Kim Peterson, Mai-Anh Peterson, Patrice Picard, Alice Purton, Josephina Quayson, Pedro Henrique Queiroz, Brandon Rayment, Alexandra Richards, Leigh Richards, Jamie Rosso, Nida Sayeed, Alex Simons, Charlie Simpson, Aaron Singh, Antonino Sipiano, Justine Spiers, Marlon Stewart, Tom Swaine Jameson, Catherine Tolstoy, Maria Tsang, Nicola and Sarah Twiner, Frankie David Viner, Sophie Louise Viner, Nhat Han Vong, Rupert and Roxy Walton, Devika Webb, George Wheeler, Claudius Wilson, Andreas Wiseman. Kate Yudt, Tanyel Yusef.

Gratitude also to Hampden Gurney School, Walnut Tree Walk Primary School and St John the Baptist C. of E. School.

Contributors: Petra Boase, Stephanie Donaldson, Sarah Maxwell, Hugh Nightingale, Michael Purton, Thomasina Smith, Jacki Wadeson, Sally Walton.